Myself

WHEN YOUNG

Myself
WHEN YOUNG

❦❀❁❀❁❀❁❀❁❀❁❀❁❀❁❀❁❀❁❀❁❀❀

KARL DETZER

Funk & Wagnalls

NEW YORK

Copyright © 1968 by Karl Detzer
All Rights Reserved.
Library of Congress Catalog Card Number: 68-12005
Published by Funk & Wagnalls, *A Division of* Reader's Digest Books, Inc.

PRINTED IN THE UNITED STATES OF AMERICA

FAIR WARNING

THIS IS NOT HISTORY. It is merely an album of remembered characters and a retelling of unforgotten events. Any tale I set down here of persons or happenings before my own time, I am repeating as I heard it, usually from participants.

I apologize for errors. After seventy years of peace and war, Republicans and Democrats, fire and flood, forgive a fragile memory if I misspell some great-aunt's middle name, or put the behind forty of the Old Home Place in the wrong quarter section. I may even be happily careless in placing halos on certain ladies' pretty, if reckless, heads.

But of one thing I can boast. This report, reaching from my second to thirteenth year or thereabouts, is unique. Nowhere do I claim to have taught Eddie Rickenbacker to fly, Henry Ford to design his Model T, General MacArthur to win battles, or Ernie Hemingway to write masculine fiction. A couple of other fellows did that.

Two women are responsible for this volume. My mother always wanted to write a history of her home town. Better than anyone else, she knew every square yard of it, who did what, where and when, and usually why. I remember the way she listened to old men and women and hurried home to lift the silver lid of the glass inkwell on her desk, dip the blunt stub pen and set down her notes. Our yesterdays amused and excited her. But household economics and her good works among the less fortunate, always conducted in secrecy, prevented her from doing all she wished.

And my wife. This book is partly hers. Her inspiration, supplication and bulldog determination elbowed me through the task to the bitter end. This account would have been much funnier and more prone to libel laws, if I had gone my own carefree way with it. I am eternally grateful to her.

K.D.

"Myself when young did eagerly frequent
Doctor and Saint and heard great argument
About it and about: but evermore
Came out by the same door wherein I went."

—STANZA 21, *The Rubáiyát* ACCORDING TO
ST. FITZGERALD

CONTENTS

EXCITEMENT YESTERDAY

✱↬✿↬✱↬✿↬✱↬✿↬✱↬✿↬✱↬✿↬✱↬✿↬✱↬✿↬✱↬✿↬✱↬✿

FOR ANY BOY with an appetite for legends, melodrama and tales of danger, for heroic pioneers, frontier soldiers, spies and savage red men, Fort Wayne, Indiana, at the turn of the century was an exciting place to live. Remembering my boyhood there, I pity those lads forced to discover a spectacular past only from printed pages, instead of from the lips of old men and women who had waited in the wings in the closing scenes of a gaudy drama.

These tellers of adventurous tales had never shaken the firm hand of General "Mad Anthony" Wayne, who was George Washington's favorite frontier soldier, nor even met that fierce but peacemaking Miami Chief Little Turtle, the greatest Indian of them all. But their fathers or grandfathers had fought or traded with both of them and entertained both under their sod roofs—never at the same time, of course.

Indians, Frenchmen, British and finally the Americans had argued over that pinpoint of geography in what now is northeastern Indiana, which had to be held at whatever cost to protect the upper Mississippi Valley and fur-rich wilderness to the west. Here, where the St. Mary's and St. Joe Rivers join to form the muddy Maumee, the Americans had set up their strongest outpost. On a small rise of land where the rivers

merged, only a step from the center of today's city, had stood
General Wayne's tall, stout palisades and log blockhouses that
gave the settlement its name. *Kekionga,* the Miamis called it.

There had been excursions and alarums up the road from
where I sat and listened. To hear the sons and daughters of
pioneers tell it, the white hordes who tore the country from the
red man had swarmed through swamps and thickets just the
day before yesterday, and one need only a little imagination to
pick up the echo of war whoops and musket shots.

The last traces of the forts had disappeared long before I
burst on the scene in 1891, but on the site of Wayne's blockhouses the city maintained a small sodded triangle with a
cannon mounted on a marble base, to remind us of all we
owed the general and his ragged troops. Every spring and
summer the ladies of the D.A.R. planted fresh flowers around
the marble slab, and if there were a ceremony, I made sure I
attended. If I could escape with it, I carried under my arm my
father's prized walking stick, a nondescript, overlong staff
whittled from a log out of the last blockhouse.

There had been several forts, first French, then American,
on or near the small plot, the last of them built by that re-
nowned Indian fighter, Major John Whistler. As years passed
and even the oak timbers crumbled, the town was platted, and
cabins, then small brick houses, rose where a little while
before stockades had kept back unfriendly savages. The first
house I remember living in as a child stood on the site of
Wayne's fort. Somewhere between our front steps and the
middle of East Berry Street, fifty feet away, had been the
southeast blockhouse.

My Grandfather Goshorn, an exacting man, as behooved a
surveyor and civil engineer, after careful measurements and
consultation of old records set up his transit one day and
placed the corner of the blockhouse on the short red-brick
walk leading down from our porch steps. His good friend,
City Engineer Frank Randall, disagreed with him. Mr. Randall, who thought that all important historical landmarks
properly belonged on public domain, argued that the corner of
the blockhouse had been somewhere near the middle of the

street. Grandfather won. His transit, compass and link chain were every bit as accurate as Mr. Randall's, so he marked the spot on a brick in his own walk.

To live on a site of history was not new to my family. My mother, born at Shade Gap, Pennsylvania, a few years after the Civil War, told us how in her childhood her family had described the roar of battle, coming up from the southeast, from Culp's Hill, Little Round Top and Cemetery Ridge, as Longstreet, Sickles, Meade, Pickett, Pettigrew, Trimble and Lee charged and countercharged, and obscure men died bravely for the North and for the South.

My father's birthplace was on what had been the parade ground at Fort Defiance, General Wayne's earlier northwestern Ohio stronghold, some fifty miles downstream from our town, at the strategic point where the Maumee met the Auglaize. In the late 1850s, he had played with his brothers in the rifle pits and over the earthworks and broken logs of old Fort Defiance.

"They made good firewood if you didn't mind a lot of smoke," he used to tell us, "so people too lazy to cut and dry good oak tore out the logs and burned them."

There were stories nearer home, told by participants or relayed by others who could recognize a lively tale when they heard it, whether or not they could make all its details fit together. Men and women, reputable ancients like Mr. David Comparet or Mrs. Ed Colerick, the gray-haired *grande dame* of the Colerick household, described the past for anyone who would listen. Grandpa Comparet, in his white-painted brick house on Liberty Street, near what was left of the Wabash and Erie Canal, had robust tales of his wife's father, Captain Dana Columbia, "the best damn canaler of them all." He always pronounced it "ca*nal*-er," not "ca*nawl*-er," as New York Staters did on the big Erie ditch.

Eagle-beaked Captain Columbia had been the elegant, hard-knuckled master of the packet *Chief Richardville*, hauling passengers and freight through the new canal that paralleled the portage and later supplanted it, only in the end to be supplanted itself by the Nickel Plate Railroad. The Comparets represented the French influence in our early Great Lakes country. Their shrewd father had come down to General Wayne's territory from the north with the fur traders, and when the tow path was ready, he got together a boat and a pair of horses and showed less ambitious folk how to make and invest money. Comparets also always had style; their men knew how to bow to the ladies, and their women were beautiful.

Aged Mrs. Colerick, rocking in her black-walnut chair in her daughter's house on West Wayne Street, a thin, plain, positive woman with hair parted squarely in the middle, reconstructed for me her girlhood down by the river. She was the only person I knew who had been born in the old fort. Her father, as treasurer, had handled what money the new county could scrape together; and her husband later gave the town its first public bathhouse, so poorer whites could smell clean all winter and in summer need not plunge into the river for a Sunday bath. She told how Ed Colerick had sat on the early grand juries, stern bodies of citizens who believed in law and order, and fined a man twenty-five cents for stepping where he shouldn't step or three dollars for selling liquor illegally to either Indian or white.

Some of her stories had come down to her from her friend Laura Suttenfield, who had lived inside the stockades when the thin little garrison was Post Miami. This doughty pioneer had even known the old squaw who one day, through spite, betrayed the commandant to savages, who massacred most of the company. I was grown up before I learned that what was neatly called a "love affair" had been a spicy part of that particular story.

A number of old timers could remember that daft, kindly dreamer, Johnny Appleseed, who scattered seeds to make the wilderness bloom and possessed the good judgment to die, not far off in New York or Ohio, but in a farmhouse near the old David Archer place north of town, which gave boys of my generation a chance to dig into history and at the same time into the clay and loam of Mr. Archer's acres seeking the unmarked grave.

Naturally I hurried home with every fresh batch of reminiscences, often going first to my Grandfather Goshorn's tall, black-walnut desk in the corner of his bedroom to check the geography. As a surveyor and engineer, this grandfather loved the land and all that this implied—not so much for its history, as I happened to at the moment and as my mother did always—but because the land itself breathed and lived to him, and he knew how its contours and its rivers controlled men's lives. As a county official, he had his office in the Court House, but his detailed work he brought home to the uninterrupted quiet of his room. His desk stood under a window, and from the ceiling over it a gas lamp with its brand-new Welsbach mantle threw a sharp, white light.

Here, after long days in the field, from which he returned tired and muddy, leaving his boots on the back porch, he scrubbed his hands and carefully registered his official findings, working with slide rule and drawing compass, T-square and tri-square, filling a scratch pad with figures in columns that he, at least, could understand. There was a tall stool beside the desk, but he preferred to stand in his soft romeo slippers, puffing his cigar vigorously. In the immense drawer under the smooth, hardwood board that was the desk top, he kept county plats, township-line drawings, drainage-ditch tracings, roads and paths; and across each section, quarter section and behind forty the owner's name was neatly written in a fine Spencerian hand.

On those plats I matched the names in the most recent story I had heard to roads, creeks and ditches. Come Saturday, I went exploring, out to Green Camp Spring in Pleasant Township where the Indians had liked to congregate, to Owen Hatfield's farm in Lafayette, to "Settler Sam" Dunlap's in Aboite. My Grandfather Goshorn had "dried up the malaria" in Aboite. He had been engineer for the Little River Ditch, dug through forty miles of mosquito-thick swamp, where the Wabash trains had crawled axle-deep in water. The word had not been "Aboite" originally, he explained. The French had called the river *à Bouette*, meaning "with minnows," but the Indians and trappers had corrupted it.

It was harder to find my way in Lafayette Township. Here the oak forests had once been so thick that the settlers had burned them to the ground—not for firewood, but just to get room to move around and breathe. But in open country I could consult the "witness" trees, often hidden in fence-corner brush, that Grandfather Goshorn had taught me to look for in the land descriptions. Many of them had become rotted stumps since the maps were drawn, but by careful pacing one could be fairly sure just where one was. At least I could plant my bare feet in the soil and say to myself that here I stood on the site of the frightful skirmish Mrs. Colerick or Grandpa Comparet had talked about; here deeds of heroism or cowardice, shame or patriotism had been everyday affairs.

Some Saturdays, with less enthusiastic companions, I roamed the dark and tangled wilderness of Devil's Hollow, west of town, and the still-visible tow paths of the abandoned canal, on the weed-grown railroad right of way.

The Indians and early settlers had been a careless lot, Grandfather Goshorn explained. They had scattered tools, weapons, pottery and bones all over the place, encouragement for properly constituted youths to pick up their spades years later and start digging in their back yards or on the river bank. After spring freshets subsided, we found newly uncovered arrowheads and broken bits of copper utensils downstream from the Walton Avenue Bridge or at the foot of Delaware Street, above the rocky ford where Little Turtle's warriors had scalped poor General Harmar's troops.

Harmar had not been a great general, everyone admitted. But he had been an American, hadn't he? General Wayne had sent him out to give the British and their Indian allies a good thrashing, but Harmar had become very careless with his flanks. So he got the thrashing instead of the British and the Indians, and all that came of the battle, as far as I was concerned, was an example of careless attitude, remarked upon pointedly by my mother from time to time.

The Walton Avenue Bridge was a fine, big one with a plank roadway, and like so many others in the county, my Grandfather Goshorn's name as designer could be read plainly on the plate at the top. The dozen arrowheads I found there, along with a stone tomahawk and a cup of beads, I kept in a glass case from my father's drug store, along with a beaded buckskin tobacco pouch that my grandfather had brought home from a surveying trip in "Indian country" in the West— and I made sure that any guest in the house paused to admire my amateur collection.

The professional collector in my acquaintance was my mother's friend Mr. Jacob Dunn, Indiana's distinguished historian. His bloody volume, *Massacres of the Mountains,* was one of my favorite books, and it was a great holiday when he invited me to go exploring with him. He was a gentle, hulking, pipe-smoking, seemingly very old man—about forty-five— who strained tremendously interesting conversation through a mustache of heroic proportions as he scrambled across briar patches and wet ground.

From him I learned that history was no mere collection of names and dates printed on pages in a book. It was a swamp where your feet sank into deep Indiana muck; or a sandbar across a creek; or a trail winding through willow thickets to what looked like an ordinary low hump of earth; or a faint, narrow path zigzagging up to a high point where, after you got your breath, you saw down below, not just the prosperous new red barns with their Mail Pouch Tobacco signs, but the glorious past that helped erect them. He showed me what evidence to seek and how to distinguish between a mound of earth made accidentally by a fallen log and a true earthen structure created by men's hands.

The buckboard that he rented for these expeditions had room in the box behind the seat for relics he hoped to bring back. At some point near the site of the day's exploration, usually among the earthworks on either side of the St. Joe River or Leo Creek, ten or fifteen miles from town, he would tie the horse by a long rope to a willow where there was a stand of grass to eat and go forward afoot, lugging his tools in a soiled, old carpetbag.

Preserving historic evidence was every bit as important as discovering it in the first place, Mr. Dunn explained. He showed me how to dig—carefully, always carefully—into the side rather than the top of a mound, watching the strata appear and sifting each small spadeful of overturned sand. His eyes, squinting through his heavy lenses, watched endlessly for bits of bone, flint chips, crockery shards. Some days he found a few, some days none; and always he went home reluctantly, assuring my mother when we arrived that once more we hadn't been scalped.

The few Indians remaining in our region were not the scalping kind. They never had been. The two whose acquaintance I tried to develop both were members of the proud Miami Tribe, descendants of the handful left behind when the government moved most of them West. They not only had no scalps to hang on their tepees, they had no tepees; and they were not even the type that Artists Remington and Catlin liked to paint. They were just Indians, in my case one woman and one man, cast in no heroic mold at all, though the lady had claim to the title of Princess. But they were alive and close enough to see and speak to, and that was all that mattered.

The lady, it developed, didn't care whether she spoke to me or not. Her name, *Kil-so-quah,* was not as intriguing to me as her first husband's. He had been known around the countryside as Mr. John Owl, and a son of another of her mates was White Loon. But she was a bona fide Princess, the granddaughter of the great Chief Little Turtle, and she was supposed to have stories of him that I wanted to hear.

So one summer day, after spending the night at Mr. Tom Ellison's farm, an enchanting place with the semi-Indian name of *Mondamin Meadow*—where I ate too much watermelon for breakfast—I walked nine dusty miles down the Huntington Plank Road, from which most of the planks had disappeared, to the village of Roanoke. There I came to the Princess' castle, a dingy little house, its windows stuffed with rags, set in a patch of tall weeds. It was rumored that she had been born around 1810, so the day I forced myself on her she was perhaps ninety years old, tall like Little Turtle, but unlike him, very fat. Her dress was ragged calico, not particularly sanitary, her face a mass of contending wrinkles, her hair unbrushed.

She was smoking a long, black stogie and refused to put it down to talk; and I learned nothing new of Chief Little Turtle.

"Do you remember him?"

Silence.

"Do you have relics I could see?"

Silence.

If one wanted to converse with *Kil-so-quah,* I discovered, one spoke Miami and then only when spoken to.

My second Indian had good manners, in spite of the fact that he was related to her. He was John Godfrey, known in our community as Chief Godfrey, even after he joined the Elks Lodge and served honestly and faithfully, if not spectacularly, as a round-faced, slow-motion, quiet patrolman in the Fort Wayne Police Department who said "Good morning" civilly to everybody. Chief Godfrey—the title was honorary for all male descendants of Little Turtle—dwelt those years on the ancestral reserve southwest of town near the County Poor Farm, as our home for the indigent was callously called.

This was not too appropriate an environment for a direct descendant of rich Jean Baptiste de Richardville, I thought. Richardville—my generation learned early to pronounce it properly, "Reesh-ar-veel"—was the son of a titled French trader and a sister of Little Turtle, whom he followed as chief of the Miamis. He had been born in a hut across the river from the fort in an old apple orchard where, when I was roaming about, one shrivelled tree still stood. An Indian sharpshooter supposedly had perched in its branches during one battle until a shot from the fort brought him down.

Horatio Alger never used Trader Richardville as an early example of "poor-boy-makes-good," but he easily could have. For as soon as the settlers and "savages" stopped shooting at each other, Richardville rapidly became the wealthiest Indian in the West, profiting from what the Supreme Court now might call a monopoly. Before the canal was built, the portage or "carrying place," ten miles west of the old fort, was the shortest overland route from the Great Lakes and St. Lawrence River to the Mississippi. Any and all goods—furs, flour, powder and lead and bolts of shoddy calico—that had to be

freighted, the canny Richardville hauled. His money, chiefly in
gold, he kept in an iron-bound, oaken safe on four iron wheels.
Even empty it must have weighed a quarter ton; I once tried
to push it across the floor after it was brought to the Court
House relic room.

Richardville had fled to the British in 1812. But after his
return, the Americans apparently forgave him; for fifty years
before I was born, appreciative citizens buried him with
military honors in an old cemetery in the south portion of
Cathedral Square. For a time his monument stood there, but it
was gone before I became fascinated with history. The site
was in our neighborhood, and many a hot, summer afternoon I
walked back and forth over the dry sod behind Bishop Joseph
Rademacher's old red-brick residence, giving my imagination
full rein. Here, within sight and sound of all the wagons and
carriages rolling peacefully along Clinton Street, lay an authentic pioneer who had helped make history.

The grave of his ancestor Little Turtle was harder to find.
According to rumor—later proved true—this fearless warrior,
who bloodied some of the white man's best generals before he
was tamed, had been buried in the contentious year of 1812 in
the marsh and sand hills of what was later Mr. Abe Barnett's
farm, across the St. Mary's from the village around the fort.
Laid away with him, supposedly, was the sword with solid-
gold hilt presented to him in person by General George
Washington, as reward for his finally bringing peace between
the tribes he controlled and the "Great White Father."

I searched hard. I did not find the grave; but others did,
much later, shortly before World War I. Workmen digging a
foundation turned up the relics—Little Turtle's tomahawk,
rusted pistol, bullet mold, even the famous golden sword.

I did find the burial place of Johnny Appleseed—not the
individual grave, but a point that I knew was within a few feet
of it. Unlike Richardville, Johnny Appleseed not only had no
money, but he was in the happy predicament of having no
desire for cash, except to buy Bibles. These, and apple seeds
that he salvaged from Pennsylvania cider mills, he passed out

free, along with Christian advice, to sinners all through the lonely middle country.

If a settler, overwhelmed by such generosity, insisted on pressing a bit of silver into Johnny's soiled palm, he accepted it "for the Lord." Never for shoes for himself. Winter and summer he padded his way barefoot—or sometimes with a single shoe, one story went, because he had got an idea from somewhere that the Bible recommended one—in sand, snow, nettles or poison ivy, wearing cast-off clothes, eating only nuts and acorns, buds and berries, never meat. The Bible forbade this, too, he said. You must not kill, and that included rattlesnakes. Nor did he ever sleep in a bed—a settler's mud hearth was comfortable and warm. And why bathe?

Papers in the Court House recorded that Johnny—his real name was Jonathan Chapman—had been laid to rest, like the good Christian he was, in the Archer burying ground. The name Archer was familiar. This family had come early, was hard working and far seeing. In all the settlements springing up in the West, the first, even if faint, signs of industry to follow were the grist mills, brick kilns and sawmills. The crude kiln on the Archer farms had supplied most of our town's first bricks, and from the Archer sawmill had come one of the stories handed down to my generation. Interestingly, it concerned a boy.

The machinery needed for this first sawmill had to be fetched from Ohio, so men in the Archer family traveled east with a wagon with six yoke of oxen to haul back the boiler; horses could handle the rest of the machinery. Part way home, the wagon with the boiler got stuck in the mud; and a fourteen-year-old was sent back alone through wild, swampy country filled with savage men and animals to bring two more yoke—all this while Jackson still was President.

According to the records, the Archer burying ground lay between the Feeder Canal and Spy Run Creek, so one Sabbath morning when I should have been more properly employed, I crawled through weeds hunting Archer markers. I found them after an hour, half a dozen stubs with the name

clearly visible. So, if this were the Archer plot, Johnny Appleseed lay somewhere near by.

I led a group of amateur local historians to the spot and
showed them my find. One of them, ignoring a young brat,
gave the story to the *Evening News,* calling it his own
discovery.

When my mother a few months later announced the un-
earthing of a General Wayne spoon mold, she credited it fairly
to Plumber Anson MacPhail, who had dug it up while working
on a water line in the yard of our old house on East Berry
Street. It was a mold of bronze, in two snug-fitting parts that
together formed a lip into which to pour hot metal. On the
underside of the long handle were stamped the letters "GEN
WAYNE."

It had lain in the ground a hundred years, through wars
with Indians and British, between North and South, with the
Spaniards. And now it would rest tidily forevermore on a
museum shelf, just a plain old mold for spoons with which
hungry men had ladled up corn and beans or stirred their hot
toddies. It was an exciting discovery, I thought. I was nine
years old. The next year would end General Wayne's tumultu-
ous century and begin another.

"Fin-de-siècle," I heard someone say. The words were new
to me. They sounded interesting. I asked my mother what they
meant.

Translating loosely but with fervor, she said, "The-End-of-
the-Nineteenth-Century-Thank-God."

2

GRANDFATHER ADAM,
MARTIN LUTHER
AND THE POPE

A WORLD-WIDE GULF separated my two grandfathers. Compared with these ancestors of mine, oil and water do mix and the lion and lamb lie down cozily together. No two men could have been less alike. Their only trait in common was that they were exciting to have around, in enormously different ways. My mother's father, Bill Goshorn, the civil engineer, was more amusing by far; my father's father, the Rev. Johann Adam Detzer, was more spectacular in speech, appearance and prejudices.

Grandfather Adam was a God-fearing, Pope-hating preacher who could let children strictly alone. The two men never agreed on anything, including whether it was raining at the moment or which way was north. But they never argued openly before my mother, who disliked all wrangling at any age.

Grandfather Bill was a regular member of the household. When occasionally, for a day or month, Grandfather Adam was a guest, the two remained meticulously polite to one another. To that end, neither mentioned Grover Cleveland or William McKinley; and since these hearty forebears had violently opposed political convictions and usually considered it their patriotic duty to express them, this restraint amounted to heroic self-denial.

In Fort Wayne, with more than forty thousand people then, where every other man on the street called my mother's father "Bill," no one called Grandfather Detzer "Adam." Even had his name been William, only a person lacking in fine perception would have called him anything but the Reverend William, or better yet, Der Herr Prediger Wilhelm.

Grandfather Adam was the older of the two men by several decades. He had slipped out of his *Vaterland* one dark night about 1845 to escape the goose step and military overlords; but after fifty years in the United States, he remained an unreformed and unassimilated Bavarian. From the day in Philadelphia when he staggered off a leaky, three-masted ship after eight weeks of Atlantic storms—saved only by the intervention of Divine Providence in response to Grandfather's prayers—and somehow got himself through the bear-infested mountains into northwest Ohio, he cherished one modest ambition. That was to gather all mankind into the True Faith that he had received straight from Jehovah—and when Jehovah and this grandfather teamed up they were unbeatable.

In the village of Defiance, he began the saddlesore life of a missioner on horseback. As a member of a Lutheran fundamentalist minority among the Catholics of Munich, he had embraced the comfortable doctrine that no question of either morality or belief had two sides. So he never hesitated to contradict sinners or point out any error, great or small, in matters of theology, piety, ethics, faith, truth, the gospel according to Martin Luther, the comparative values of Berghoff versus Centlivre beer—or even the prowess of Mr. Frank Chance, the peerless first baseman of the Chicago Cubs.

Grandfather Adam hated the Devil and holy water with equal vigor, because the Good Book told him to hate the Devil and because holy water came from Rome. In fact, were he forced to choose bedfellows, he probably would have embraced Satan before the Pope. Yet for reasons so obscure that his family never even tried to explain them, he lived on cozy terms with northern Indiana's two Catholic bishops, and with

Monsignor John Oechtering of St. Mary's Catholic Church. To hear the good Monsignor and my grandfather conversing by lamplight over small glasses of wine, in what they imagined hopefully was English, was as good as a front-row seat with Weber and Fields—except, of course, that the two gentlemen of the cloth had to struggle along without the shapely benefit of Miss Lillian Russell.

Bishop Herman Alerding, whose stately, if slightly smoke-stained, Victorian residence was just down the street, also often talked at length with my grandfather; but those conversations usually were conducted in German. The Bishop was much the younger, so he always treated the older preacher with respect, even when Grandfather's prejudices shocked him into outbursts of silence. Many afternoons with nothing better to do, I tagged the two men as they strolled in the fluttering shade of apple trees in the small, old orchard separating the Cathedral from the Bishop's first dusty, red-brick palace. They argued loudly, enunciating distinctly, for each wanted the Creator to hear him and understand.

But they always shook hands in the end, after which, to Grandfather's immense revulsion, the good Bishop bestowed on him in parting a sort of informal blessing with three rather loose waves of three fingers of his right hand. At this the Reverend Adam invariably pounded the Catholic earth under his feet with his ebony cane; and once, to the Bishop's astonishment, I saw him shake the cane at the Cathedral. He then would stamp home in a black fret.

By rights he should have been a tolerant man, if a mixed inheritance is of any value. The story was handed down with circumspection and evasion, but the facts are that the direct ancestor of this German Lutheran grandfather was a Frenchman named Dubois, who as a young man had gone to Paris, studied philosophy, then medicine, and become a famous obstetrician. Bonaparte chose him as surgeon for Marie Louise, an assignment that he handled so successfully, according to an early *Britannica*, that the Emperor made him a member of the staff of savants who accompanied him to Egypt and later bestowed on him the title of General.

When the Emperor sent this favorite on an errand across the
Rhine, he met in an obscure German village the daughter of
the *Burgomeister*. They fell in love. But her father, a righteous
man, refused to recognize the compact. Dubois was French
and a Catholic, the girl German and a Lutheran. She fled with
him to Paris, but soon, on the march to Russia, her general
died. Back she went to her German village.

"I'll take you in," her father said, "if never again I hear the
name of Dubois. The child will carry his mother's name. He
will be a Lutheran." So Adam Detzer was born, and named.

Grandfather Adam had founded the first Lutheran church
in Defiance, where he preached his first sermon in an old
school building in the winter of 1851. Within a month he had
rounded up twenty-nine obedient and God-fearing settlers for
communion, many of them riding in oxcarts or walking the
muddy river bank. In the first year, as an example to all who
might follow him, he established fourteen mission posts, ford-
ing swollen streams on horseback in the spring, crossing on
tricky ice in winter, often pushing his tired but helpless mount
as much as forty hock-deep miles in fifteen Sabbath hours.
Before his missionary career was over, the churches he had
established numbered fifty-four, with congregations extending
into the Northwest Territory.

If necessary, this zealot could deliver three, four or five
hearty sermons in a day, in barn, shed, school or crossroad
store. But he preferred only two, for when he got wound up
and the Spirit of the Lord was in him, he could assail both the
Devil and the communicants for as long as three inspired
hours at a time, forgetting—or not caring—that the hardwood
planks on which the faithful squirmed had neither back rests
nor seat pads.

His was the only hymnal in the community, so he would
read each stanza aloud in his harsh Bavarian German for the
congregation to repeat, choosing a tune to suit his sometimes
vagrant fancy. In his upper vest pocket he carried a tin pitch
pipe as big as a pencil stub and this he would toot while his
captives, with varying degrees of success, tried to follow its

shrill tone. Other times he would lead with his violin tucked under his chin over a big handkerchief.

Money for himself did not matter. When, about 1900, the new auto manufacturers decided to sell a car for six hundred dollars—"a price people certainly could afford to pay"—my father mentioned for comparison that Grandfather Adam's first year's salary, according to his diary, was $101.80, most of it doled out in potatoes, cordwood, hay, a quarter of beef or as many eggs as he could carry in his saddle bags. The highest annual pay he ever received from the Defiance church in any of twenty faithful years was $385, and it wasn't all earned by preaching. In 1854, when cholera raged for three months, there sometimes were four funerals a day, with the coffin-maker, gravedigger and Grandfather hauling the bodies on a two-wheeled dray to a hastily plowed field; farmers, frightened of the plague, refused to help.

In his older years, Grandfather's physical appearance caused passersby to glance at him twice. At times the sight was so hard to believe that strangers were known to turn and walk past him a second time to make sure their eyes had not deceived them. This reverend gentleman was about five feet, five inches tall atop the rather low heels of his black romeos. His square head and short neck were set solidly on square, broad shoulders, giving him the fey aspect of one of the more personable Harz Mountain elves in the works of the Brothers Grimm. The oblong lenses in his spectacles, which he wore far down on his nose, heightened the resemblance.

His hair had begun to thin when I first knew him, but he kept it brushed down neatly except for a single lock at the rear, which stuck up like a turkey's tail feathers. The hair had refused to whiten completely, as it should have done for a man in his eighties, and was speckled here and there with strands of tawny brown. Like Grandfather himself, it seemed to reject any and all change.

His nose was ample, slightly cleft, and flared into magnificent nostrils through which, when the mood was on him, he liked to snort disdainfully—a sound effect heard easily through closed doors and across a busy street. A deeply shadowed wrinkle above his nose joined his full thicket of eyebrows, which to his death remained dark and bushy. In that era of fancy whiskers, he was clean-shaven, leaving plenty of room for his mouth, which he usually compressed between thin lips. But it was a mouth of such generous horizontal proportions that it might have been sculptured with a broad-ax. To call that vast mouth merely positive is a great injustice. It was both decisive and dogmatic, the kind of mouth entirely proper for this no-holds-barred, hell-fire, damn-the-Pope theologian, whose resemblance to Martin Luther, in one of Luther's less hilarious moods, was startling.

Even when I was very young, I knew that my Grandfather Adam and Martin Luther looked exactly alike. This was because in an uncle's drug store—the uncle's name was also Martin—I was able to observe them side by side, Grandfather Adam in the flesh and Martin Luther in a graven image.

This drug-store uncle, who too often made whimsical purchases of merchandise that could not possibly sell even at half-cost, one holiday season had paid cash for fifteen dozen foot-tall plaster busts of Luther, tastefully finished in bronze paint. The face was twisted into precisely the expression of righteous fury that Luther undoubtedly wore as he heaved his famous inkwell at the Devil. In spite of Uncle Martin's insistence that all good men were aching for such beautiful works of ecclesiastical art, my father warned him that the purchase was unwise and would be with him for a long time. For the neighborhood on which the store depended had recently been infiltrated by the Irish, come to help the expanding Pennsylvania Railroad lay its double track, and they had brought with them from the Emerald Isle just as many prejudices against Luther and all his works as Grandfather Adam had brought preferences for him.

Uncle Martin didn't believe it. He thought such talk was lunacy and blamed it on the fact that Father had disgraced himself by marrying a Presbyterian and could not be trusted in any matter concerning German Lutheran theology. So Uncle Martin went ahead and decorated the show windows

facing Calhoun Street with two rows of identical Martin
Luthers, glowering at the world in bronze and plaster fury,
supported in the back by cardboard cut-outs for Scott's Emul-
sion and Mrs. Pinkham's splendid remedy for women's woes.

A few dedicated Christians availed themselves of the bar-
gains as a religious duty, but most of the stock remained
unsold, a drug on the drug-store market. Consequently, for
many years, in whichever direction one looked in the store or
in the back room with its whiskey barrels waiting to be used in
dispensing prescriptions, Luther glowered back fiercely.

Dead ringers as Luther and this grandfather were for one
another in flesh and bone, Adam Detzer was a much more
interesting, one might almost say picturesque, character. For
one thing, so far as brief research indicates, Luther never wore
earrings. At least the plaster busts did not show any. But six
days each week Grandfather Adam wore a single heavy gold
ring with a chaste design engraved along its bottom edge,
through the hole pierced in the lobe of his left ear. The other
ear remained free. This detracted seriously from the old man's
ministerial aspect; in fact, it lent him the naughty look of an
elderly Teutonic Captain Kidd. Sabbath mornings, however,
in the front row or the pulpit, he dispensed with the single
large ring. He may have felt that it was a bit gaudy for a house
of worship. At any rate when he went to church, he wore a
pair of small, thin circlets of fine gold, one in each ear.

Some member of my family came up years later with a silly
explanation that such an unusual taste in jewelry was because
the good pastor had fallen prey to the superstition that an
earring would ward off head colds. He had done nothing of
the kind. He fortified himself against colds, pneumonia, lung
fever and kindred ills with a dollop of hot rum, sweetened
with two lumps of sugar, like any other sensible citizen; and
he wore the earring because he liked earrings. It was as simple
as that.

His lapel buttons he wore, church or no church. On the left
lapel of his long black broadcloth ministerial coat, he
espoused causes close to his heart and since Luther was
closest, he usually sported a dignified gold medal depicting

The Founder in profile. But for a time, during the war with
Spain, he substituted a much larger celluloid shield with the
slogan, "Remember the *Maine.*"

Grandfather followed his own advice by keeping the *Maine*
in mind most of his waking hours, saying long prayers for the
souls of all brave sailors who died in the *Maine* explosion, and
other prayers condemning to the lowest, hottest German Lutheran hell the beasts who set off the dynamite. His age may
have been responsible, but somehow he seemed to confuse the
Spanish War with the Spanish Inquisition. The Inquisition, to
hear him tell it, had occurred only yesterday. No punishment
was severe enough to repay those haughty Spaniards for their
cruelty to the fine Christians who remained loyal to the
German princes. In these prayers, morning and night, he
sometimes mixed the reigning Alfonso XIII, who was not
particularly bright, with that bloodthirsty fanatic Torque-
mada, the Grand Inquisitor. Certainly the good Lord would
help our brave American Boys-in-Blue to butcher this pig of a
Spanish monk and all his bodyguards.

After the glory of San Juan Hill and Manila Bay had
chastised the enemy to some extent, Grandfather removed the
picture of the *Maine* from his lapel; and later in the autumn,
he substituted a color portrait of "Our Peerless Leader," Mr.
William McKinley, wearing a noble, if slightly pompous,
expression. Crowded in beside him on the same celluloid
button was McKinley's Vice-President, Mr. Garret Augustus
Hobart of Paterson, N.J., a fierce advocate of sound business
methods. Mr. Hobart also was distinguished by a splendid
sweep of oversized dark mustache that made up in part for
Mr. McKinley's naked upper lip.

Grandfather's long, black coat was practical as well as
decorative. Its right-hand side pocket was large enough to
hold his Bible and the Lutheran *Kleine Katechismus,* which
was one of The Founder's less colorful works, plus a packet of
Smith Bros. Cough Drops, a beer-bottle opener and occasionally a handful of apples and a chunk of robust cheese wrapped
in a copy of the *Abendpost.* Across his slightly potbellied
front, vest pocket to vest pocket, looped a silver watch chain

capable of towing a laden coal barge through churning seas. It connected his silver watch and key on the right side with his heavy four-bladed pocket knife on the left. The three-inch blade, which was the longest and most lethal looking, he used for sharpening pencils and slicing the apples and cheese.

The left-hand side pocket of the long coat held Grandfather Adam's handkerchief. This was a sheet of linen slightly smaller than a mainsail, wrapped neatly around a straight razor, shaving mug, brush and strop, and a bottle of witch hazel. Since he shaved daily and never could be quite sure where God would have him stay the night, he wanted the tools handy.

The two flaring pockets often gave the coat a bushy appearance, as if he might be wearing a badly fitted bustle. Under it a royal-purple satin vest with fine vertical pleats stretched up from below his waist to the bottom edge of his reversed clerical celluloid collar. The vest, like the collar, buttoned behind. To call it impressive is to do it poor justice, for it was the sort of garment a court chamberlain might have saved for occasions of special pomp. Indoors and out, he wore a purple skull cap. It had style and, like his coat, was practical. It not only fitted close to his thin hair to protect him from winter drafts, but it rose some three inches above his head. It was edged by a heavy seam, fashioned to suggest, but not quite create, a square top, under which he sequestered important documents and interesting clippings.

The cap was satin like the vest, but no one should get the idea from talk of satin and such frivolities that Grandfather Adam was womanish in any degree. Nothing could be farther from the truth. The tough old man was about as effeminate as that pair of red-blooded citizens, Mr. John L. Sullivan and Mr. Jake Kilrain, who a few years earlier had made Richburg, Mississippi, immortal by fighting seventy-two bare-knuckled rounds and then walking out of the ring. Mr. Sullivan won, and Mr. Kilrain lived. Likewise, anyone reckless enough to make an improper remark about what Grandfather wore or said would live, but he could expect a quick lesson in manners. A handsome, ebony walking stick with a golden duck's head for a handle could serve several purposes. The duck had a sharp beak, and this man of God used it effectively more than once to clobber sinners, unbelievers and anyone else who seriously offended him. Never, I am thankful to say, on any of his grandchildren.

The earrings, lapel buttons and purple vest were only part of the ministerial costume certainly unique among Protestant clergy in those simple days. Of course, a couple of generations later, Mrs. Aimee Semple McPherson of Hollywood did a pretty good job with flowing robes, plastic angel wings and spotlights; but Grandfather Adam would have spurned her. He considered it sacrilege for any woman to try to preach in the first place, but dressing up like an angel would have been more than the old man could take. He denied it when pressed, but he didn't much care for women anyway. And for actresses not at all.

So to my mother's delight, my father's rather startled amusement, and Uncle Martin's Christian horror, Grandfather was discovered late one Saturday afternoon leaving the Temple Theatre by a side exit that was directly across East Wayne Street from the Rev. Samuel Wagenhals' study window. The crusading Mr. Wagenhals recently had been thundering from his pulpit in Trinity English Lutheran Church, which also frowned across the street at the theatre, against what he considered its indecent entertainment. Attendance by any church member was forbidden.

Grandfather was in the highest spirits when he got home, swinging the ebony cane almost jauntily. The bad news had arrived ahead of him, brought in person by Uncle Martin, who was out of breath. Of course he had gone to the theatre, Grandfather admitted without even clearing his throat. Why not?

What was more, he had been honored. When he went to the box office and put down a quarter to buy a seat in the balcony, the manager, Mr. Frank Stouder, pushed the money back at him and pressed on him a one-dollar ticket, absolutely free, for the stage box on the right-hand side. Why? In deference to his reversed collar, no doubt, Grandfather said.

He had greatly enjoyed the matinee performance of *The Hand That Dragged Her Down,* he told my mother. Too bad more people couldn't see it. Ignore Wagenhals. He belonged to the wrong synod anyway.

The story of the Reverend Adam's sin in attending the performance got out, as Uncle Martin said it would; and only firm words by the Reverend Mr. Dannecker of St. John's Lutheran and the Reverend Mr. Lange of Concordia succeeded in calming the more excitable of their fellow preachers. Later I heard my mother tell Uncle Gustave that Grandfather had shown no sign of disliking the notoriety.

The old gentleman did have certain scruples about entertainment on the Sabbath day; he never went to Sunday baseball games in Fort Wayne, where he might be recognized and be a bad example to the young. What he did with Sunday afternoons in Chicago, if the Cubs were playing, was his own affair. When Methodists there started a campaign against Sunday baseball, it only whetted his interest in his favorite team—he would have gone twice on a Sunday had the opportunity offered, just as he always seemed to refuse fish and double his meat-eating on Fridays.

In Fort Wayne, Grandfather attended all weekday games of the Central League, the Class B organization which in those days spread across a half-dozen mid-American States. He always managed to get to town for the openers and always complained bitterly about the quality of the baseball. In particular, he was made unhappy by the players from Evansville, Indiana, Grand Rapids, Michigan, and Wheeling, West Virginia. They were even worse, he said, than the lazy Chicago White Stockings. But in the shabby, wooden stands down near our county jail, he fell in with interesting characters; and before the game was over, he usually had nicked them for a few dollars to patch the roof of a needy church.

One day, arriving in very good spirits, he took off his purple skull cap and withdrew from inside it a packet of letters tied up in a string. These had to do, he explained to my mother, with the money he was raising to help a church with a leaky roof down at Holgate, Ohio. Not a man to laugh heartily or often, he guffawed now with satisfaction. A couple of hours ago, waiting in the Wabash station for the train to Fort Wayne, he had wangled a back-sliding skinflint he never had seen before into giving five times what Grandfather had hoped to get. The fellow might wonder when he got home what had happened to his senses, but that made it all the funnier.

If a man gave to the cause—Grandfather never asked a woman; she wasn't supposed to carry money—it didn't matter how they met or how the money had been made. The reputable Fort Wayne citizen, who for years presided over both faro and chuck-a-luck games in his high-class, but strictly illegal, establishment above a Calhoun Street business house, became a fast friend, simply because Grandfather met him on a streetcar and before they got to the Transfer Corner, nicked him for three dollars for a church at Napoleon, Ohio.

Another with whom Grandfather Adam remained for years on most intimate terms was Mr. Jimmy Summers, the jolly publican who not only tended bar in his own respectable saloon next door to Uncle Martin's drug store, but kept it respectable by tossing troublemakers from the Pennsy Railroad boiler shops out into the street. He also was president of the Friendly Sons of St. Patrick.

Grandfather Adam undoubtedly had designs on Mr. Summer's soul, just as he did on Bishop Alerding's. With pure mercenary intent, he also developed the friendship of the conductors on the city streetcar lines and all the railroads that filled Fort Wayne with roundhouses and classification yards— the important Pennsylvania and just as important Wabash, the Nickel Plate, famous for its freight, the Grand Rapids and Indiana that in a westward-moving civilization was the only one running north and south; even the two feeder lines, the Lake Shore and Michigan Southern, and the Lake Erie and Western. Grandfather Adam rode them all and bestowed his blessings on all the crews. He didn't even omit the men on the C.H.& D., the little branch that called itself the Findley, Fort Wayne and Pacific and never got an inch nearer the Pacific than Fort Wayne.

This cultivation of friendship was necessary, because though he started every year safely enough with the churchman's annual passes, he made an annual habit of losing them. By early February they were gone, lost no doubt among the papers in his skull cap. For the rest of the year, God and the conductors all willing, he rode wherever he wanted to go, no questions asked. It was easier for a tired conductor not to argue.

Grandfather gave up his last permanent charge when he was about seventy and spent the rest of his life visiting the homes of his seven sons, never with any warning of his arrival. He usually brought gifts, often a basket of eggs from the last farm on which he had spent the night. His arrival also brought instant parental warnings. Before each meal Mother would herd the younger generation into the pantry and warn sternly that, as everyone well knew, Grandfather Adam did not expect any child to talk at table unless first spoken to.

Also, Betty and Kinny, our fox terriers, must be locked in the basement. Grandfather must be spared the indignity of having to eat in a room full of *verdampten Hunde!* Naturally we resented this ukase. It not only was unreasonable, but in my sister Dorothy's mind particularly, it was bitterly unkind. More than once, even without being excused, she left the table and went and sat on the cellar steps with the dogs.

The animals gone, Grandfather Adam, snorting through his nose, would glower around the table to make sure all dirty, little hands were folded, all tousled heads bowed, before he launched into his dissertation to the Lord. Naturally he prayed in German, so that we children came to think of God as bilingual, issuing His commands either in German or in English with a Bavarian accent. We also were convinced that God must look a lot like both Grandfather and the busts of Martin Luther, and the fact that our mother was a Presbyterian, who when half-orphaned had spent a few years in a convent, only served to confuse us more.

Most preachers who visited our table were content with a simple invocation. Dr. David Moffat of the First Presbyterian Church could say all that was needed in a dozen slow words. Only the Reverend Pastor Sihler, who appeared occasionally with Grandfather—they had planted Lutheran stakes of Zion together in northwestern Ohio in their inspired young manhood—shared the glory by pronouncing a benediction that was even longer than Grandfather's invocation. There also were times, if the conversation bored him, when Grandfather would interrupt any course, or even a half-uttered sentence, for an extra interlude of pious conversation with on high.

We managed usually to stay obediently silent throughout the meal. But should we not, our visiting Grandfather without warning would bring his broad, flat hand down on the table with a bang that made dishes and silverware jump, and bellow, "Halt!" It was a German *Halt!* full of the echoes of Prussian howitzers. We halted.

I could not have been more than five years old the day I was really proud of the Reverend Adam. His friend Jimmy Summers, who kept the "respectable" saloon, as a professional Irishman divided the year into St. Patrick's Day and three hundred and sixty-four ordinary days. On March seventeenth that year I had been allowed to go with Grandfather to my uncle's drug store to see the parade, but after a few minutes the old man left me and went next door for a friendly conversation with Mr. Summers. He did that often and always came back feeling better.

This morning he did not come back, but no one missed him. Everybody lined the curb when the bands first sounded. Leading the procession came Gart Schober's men, all with green ribbons tied to their instruments, bravely struggling with "The Wearin' o' the Green." Then the Hibernian Rifles marched past in their splendid blue and white uniforms, with green rosettes pinned to their chests and green ribbons streaming from their guns.

Behind the military companies came the plain and fancy Irish of our town, in wavering ranks, row on happy row. And to my utter delight, there in the second row came my clergyman grandfather, purple vest and earring and all, arm in arm with Mr. Jimmy Summers. They were keeping step with each other, after a fashion, but ignoring the band.

Grandfather was holding aloft his ebony cane, which someone had decorated gaily for him with ribbons of green. He was waving it enthusiastically and shouting something about England being "kaput." Both he and Mr. Summers seemed extremely happy.

"Look at Grandfather!" I shouted proudly.

Uncle Martin looked and went into a swift decline. When he recovered sufficiently, he telephoned my mother.

That evening my father and his brother solemnly put Grandfather on a Wabash Railroad train for Defiance, Ohio, and thereafter they always shushed me when I mentioned the glorious day when Grandfather marched in the parade.

I was proud, too, the day of his funeral in 1903. A thousand mourners jammed St. Paul's German Lutheran Church, half a block from our house. The bell began to toll at high noon and continued its mournful ritual until the last of the carriages disappeared, the horses clumping slowly far out on Madison Street on the way to Concordia Cemetery at a quarter past four. There were two extra carriages filled with flowers.

It was a long service because seven preachers participated, including two of Grandfather Adam's minister sons. Six of his seven sons carried the casket to the grave. The congregation sang "Ein' Feste Burg" as they knew it should be sung, with stamina and conviction, and it was heard for blocks. Yes, it was heard distinctly away Up There.

We children had felt awe but no warm sense of affection for the fierce old man; perhaps it was pride that caught in our throats that overcast day when the bell tolled endlessly. At any rate we all went home to our rooms, shut the doors and had a good long cry.

3

RAILROADS, BRIDGES,
GOLD LEAF
AND RATTLESNAKES

I F THE Reverend Adam could let children strictly alone,
the other grandfather—surveyor, railroad builder, timber
cruiser, bridge designer, politician, expert pistol and rifle shot
—was an approachable person who let you know that he occasionally relished the companionship of a boy or girl.

My mother's father, whose name was William Henderson
Goshorn, lived with us from my earliest memory until his
death in 1902 or 1903. He was born in Pennsylvania, near the
Maryland line, of Holland Dutch ancestry; and he always
made it clear that this did not mean Pennsylvania Dutch, who,
he said, were not Dutch at all, but German. He did have, I am
happy to believe, a light infusion of Amsterdam Jewish blood.

When people in town called him "Bill," he responded
quickly, happily and naturally. Because county surveyors and
bridge superintendents had to be elected to their offices every
two years, he was on easy terms with every Catholic priest,
Lutheran or Methodist preacher, doctor, lawyer, grocer,
teacher, railroad employee, streetcar conductor and bartender
in town—for reasons similar to those which impelled Grandfather Adam to cultivate the friendship of train conductors.

Grandfather Goshorn also responded happily to his grandchildren. Brother Gus, the youngest member of the family,

who arrived in 1899, was the only boy baby in our neighborhood not named Dewey. Instead, later, he had to answer to
"Powder" because he resembled the baby on the Mennen
Powder box. Gus was not old enough to appreciate Grandfather
Goshorn, but the twins, Dorothy and Don, hung on his big
chair as much as I did. To Dorothy he was the source of supply
for the fragile, bisque heads of her "August dolls," named like
her brother after our father. When she broke them regularly
and, weeping, held the headless white leather sawdust-stuffed
body up for a harsh world to mourn, it was Grandfather, ignoring mother's regular edict that if she broke one more, no other
would be forthcoming, who quickly provided a beautiful, ex-
pendable new head.

This grandfather, as a young man, had driven stakes and
carried surveyor's bulky chains in Pennsylvania before venturing on into the rough buffalo country and wild Colorado. He
had built bridges in the Mississippi delta; toward the end of
his career, he laid out the Grand Rapids and Indiana Railroad
to the Straits of Mackinac, and if a bear got in his way, he shot
it. Left with a motherless daughter, he finally had shaken the
wanderlust from his boots and settled in Indiana.

He was never a sentimental man. Yet he preserved for me
the first hundred-foot chain he had used as a young surveyor.
It was heavy, with six-inch links, and one day he lifted it from
the wall and showed me where the links had worn smooth
from use. Being an engineer, he had as strong a dislike for
inaccuracy as my father did for tardiness. So he took out a
map of the state and showed me how, even if the wear on one
link amounted only to thousandths of an inch, were he to
measure straight east to west with a hundred feet of worn
chain, by the time he reached the opposite side of the state,
the measurement would be wrong by a foot or two. Later, on a
summer vacation, I handled worn chain for a surveyor not as
careful as my grandfather and could understand the occasional boundary disputes that went into court.

Topping six feet in height, Grandfather Goshorn weighed all
of two hundred and thirty pounds in wool shirt and corduroy
pants, and had a deep but not loud voice and a florid com-

plexion. His thick, unruly, reddish hair, streaked with gray when I knew him, stood up an inch or two, giving him an appearance of still more height. His reddish, never unruly beard was just long enough to cover a part of his narrow black bow tie. His steel-rimmed spectacles, with oblong lenses like Benjamin Franklin's, he always referred to as "my specs." He wore high Number-Thirteen boots, and in his bedroom he kept a black-walnut bootjack with which to pull out of them without stooping. At times he sported a small enamel American flag in his buttonhole; and for the record he was a member in good standing of the First Presbyterian Church, but he never attended services there or anywhere else, and leaned heavily toward agnosticism.

This grandfather was an outdoorsman who thought of home principally as a place to thaw out in winter and change into dry clothes, and to sit through a blistering summer afternoon with a large blue handkerchief on his head, over which he occasionally poured ice water. At home he also enjoyed hearty meals of meat and potatoes and an evening dollop of good Maryland whiskey.

I discovered early that the pockets of his working clothes were broad and deep, to accommodate such items as a Bowie knife, a silver hunting-case watch, the steel tape that had supplanted the old surveyor chains, a pencil stub, a waterproof match box, a slide rule, a compass, extra glasses, a half-dozen black cigars and a thick, leather-covered notebook. He was thoroughly American, with little interest in matters European, and my mother's interest in the wide world amused him. He did say once, in my hearing, that he thought Lorraine should be returned to France and that Poland should be free. But beyond a hope that some day he could see the St. Goddard Tunnel in Switzerland and discuss it with its builders, he had no wish to travel—he liked where he was.

The only exception to this had been his desire to look at Brooklyn's new suspension bridge. Hanging on his bedroom wall, along with some Western prints by Remington, was a framed lithograph of the bridge the Roeblings had built, cut out from *Harper's Weekly*. In the late 1880s he had gone all the way to New York for the sole purpose of seeing its sensational steel wires, and he returned to Indiana pronouncing it the most beautiful structure designed and built by man.

I kept silent when he told me this. He was usually right, but this time I knew he was wrong. The most beautiful structure in the world was the new Allen County Court House for which he had been engineer in charge of construction. Not many boys had a grandfather whose name was engraved forever in a marble cornerstone. Or for that matter on the plate at each end of dozens of bridges.

Our town boasted several elegant buildings, among them the City Hall. This cross between Milwaukee Gothic and early Victorian, for which my father's friend Sim Mahurin had been the architect, was a thing of beauty that threatens to be a joy forever, for it still stands after seventy-three years. Not because of the present trend to preserve a landmark. Rather, why should a frugal community tear down a building simply because it has gone out of style?

True, the City Hall was a majestic structure, but nothing in my eyes could match my Grandfather Goshorn's new Court House. This was a Romanesque confection of white limestone from southern Indiana's Bedford Hills, with beautiful Ionic friezes and gorgeous Doric columns, crowned with Corinthian leaves. A heroic statue of Liberty stood on its dome, which also boasted good, readable clock dials a dozen feet wide. On the facade were busts of General Anthony Wayne, George Washington, Col. John Allen, Chief Tecumseh and Chief Little Turtle.

The day its cornerstone was laid was the highlight of my young life until then. In the morning there had been a Grand Parade with Governor James Mount in the reviewing stand, and I sat on my grandfather's big lap in one of Mr. Bide Barnett's open hacks with the top down. Mr. Brentwood Tolan, the architect, and Congressman Jim Robinson rode with us, the latter talking a lot; and in front, holding the reins on the driver's box, was my friend and hero Mr. Cy Fike, with a stovepipe hat and glowing nose.

In the afternoon, right up in the front line where I could see everything, I watched all the maps, the day's newspapers and other future heirlooms go into the copper box that was to be preserved forever in the cornerstone. At the end of the program, I did not sing "America" with the other children. They were not from my school, and besides, it was much more important to be holding the hand of the great man who was superintending the construction of the building than it was to sing.

On the wall of my grandfather's room beside his first surveyor's chain, near the desk where he drew his plats, hung a gun rack, filled with cherished weapons, dustless under glass, oiled, polished, loaded and ready for instant use in a crisis. Only occasionally was there a crisis, but when it came it was a world-shaker. The first, in my experience, concerned the Court House before it was finished.

Grandfather was careful of other people's rights. He also had a blunt way of describing a man's morals. So when he discovered that the gold leaf on the new courtroom ceiling was not really gold, he used the word "thief"; and the contractor in charge of the paint job, when he heard the word, threatened vengeance on him.

It was a Sabbath morning and Grandfather and I were alone. He was in the corner of the sitting room in his big, padded easy chair with his buffalo robe spread on the floor in front of him. It had a red-flannel lining and was a blessing, he said, for tired feet. He had brought the skin home years before from Wyoming, and the round hole in the beast's right shoulder showed where his very first bullet had gone home.

I was lying on my stomach, looking at the Doré illustrations in *Paradise Lost,* the largest book in the house, when County Commissioners John Stellhorn and Matt Ferguson arrived in Matt's buckboard. Grandfather listened to their story, sighed and pulled on his boots.

"You will have to come along," he told me; "you can't stay alone." But before he put on his hat, he went upstairs and got his Western .38 revolver from the rack and secured it in his belt under his coat.

The architect and the paint-job contractor were waiting

outside the Court House. With them and the county commissioners, we climbed a ladder into the unfinished building and up a rough stairway into the courtroom. There, in the middle of the floor, Grandfather, who had been silent all the way downtown, lighted a sulphur candle. It had a vile odor, and it would blacken the ceiling if the trim were not gold. And so it did, leaving a dirty, smeary black all over the phony gilt. We ran from the smell, but to my disappointment there was no shooting. The contractor agreed to do the work over, and Grandfather went home and hung up his gun.

I did see him use it another time, but not on a contractor. Years before, in the muckland west of town some five or six miles, he had run a grid of survey lines for drainage ditches that were to flow into the headwaters of the Wabash, either through the Little River or the Eel. In the area, he later had bought sixty or eighty acres that he called his "farm." The land lay on a ridge so low that only a surveyor's instrument could pick out the highest points with any accuracy. West of the ridge it sloped away to the Mississippi River system, and to the east and north, water flowed into Lake Erie and down the St. Lawrence. So each spring most of the area became a sodden marsh, with its only dry land, known as Fox Island, rising some three or four feet out of the water. This was the center of his "farm."

A scarecrow of a man named DeWitt, who talked explosively through his nose, occupied the little frame cabin on what annually was the island, and took care of Grandfather's horse in the small barn. One Sabbath morning in early spring, he appeared, dripping, at the door of our Montgomery Street house, having waded, swum and walked a good five or six miles to bring bad news.

It was a horrendous tale of waters rising overnight, surrounding his Ararat completely, so that he had to come for help.

"Is the barn flooded?" Grandfather asked. Mr. DeWitt shook his head, speechless. "The house?" Another shake. "Then what the devil are you coming here for, dripping all over the floor?"

The poor man swallowed. "They come up from all sides," he reported. "Place was full of 'em."

"Full of what?"

"Rattlesnakes," said the farmer. "They was drove up by the high water."

"Why didn't you kill them?" Grandfather asked reasonably.

"Tried to. Too many of 'em. Was tryin' to kill 'em when they did it."

"Did what?"

"Bit your horse."

Grandfather missed a beat, then asked, "Are you sure?"

"It's dead," was the reply.

Grandfather pulled on his boots and went again to the gun rack. Hiring a rig from Mr. Barnett's barn, he drove with me standing by his knee, scared Farmer DeWitt beside him, and two long-barreled pistols on the back seat. My mother had objected to my going, but this time my grandfather, from whom she inherited her positive character, was in no mood for argument. Did she want to keep me wrapped in cotton batting all my life? I'd have to face the world sometime, and could she think of anyone better fitted to show it to me than he? He would take me, I would enjoy it, and there would be no discussion.

Borrowing a skiff from a neighboring gentleman whose name was Doswell and who didn't offer to come with us, Grandfather paddled the last mile, with me in the bow and miserable Farmer DeWitt squatting in the stern. I have a recollection of loud, rushing waters and a wonder, not entirely fearless, as to how many rattlesnakes there really would be.

Arriving at the two or three acres remaining above the flood, Grandfather pulled the skiff up on the land, made the painter fast to a stump and bade me remain in the boat, not put so much as a finger over the gunwale, and did I understand?

For so big a man, he always moved rapidly, and despite the dead horse lying outside the shed, he suddenly seemed to be enjoying himself. He fired his pistol, loaded, fired again. The bombardment certainly was the loudest occurring between Appomatox and Admiral Dewey's assault on Manila Bay.

Eleven rattlers died in one glorious half-hour. Leaving one
gun with the farmer and warning him to keep it dry and clean
and oiled and to bury the horse, Grandfather rowed back to
Mr. Barnett's horse and buggy, and delivered them to the bus
barn. We were home in time for noon dinner.

The spinster MacPhail sisters, Margaret, Jennie and Mary,
two of them teachers and one the housekeeper, liked to make
social calls on their friends in a body; and my mother was a
particular friend. The night of the rattlesnake affair, they sat
on the edges of their chairs in our sitting room, their faces
flushed with astonishment, as my mother recounted the epic
of Fox Island and Mr. DeWitt and my grandfather's trusty
pistols.

In the corner, smoking a cigar, Grandfather rested with his
feet on the buffalo robe, quietly reading yesterday's *Chicago
Inter-Ocean*. He paid no attention to the four women and
pretended not to hear them.

It was Miss Margaret, eldest of the spinsters, who seemed
most impressed by Grandfather's sharpshooting. She was a
remarkable woman whose dignity approached the condition of
majesty, and she reminded some people of a rather bony
Queen Victoria with a broad, Scotch upper lip.

Miss Margaret is the only woman I remember who refused
to have her gray, plain skirts shortened as much as an inch in
deference to the bicycle. Hers was a splendid up-to-date
Josephine model—named in honor of Mrs. Bonaparte—for
which she had paid $14.35 in one of her rare spendthrift
moments. She rode it sedately to her work as principal of the
Bloomingdale School each morning, pumping slowly and
steadily while she balanced her lunch, wrapped in last evening's newspaper, on the handlebars. On a shelf behind the
seat she carried a small library held firmly in place by a
leather strap.

"How," she asked Grandfather, in a voice full of the broad
A's that were the mark of true culture in our town, "how *cawn*
a mawn possibly kill a *raw*ttlesnake with a revolver?"

Grandfather put down his newspaper and shifted his feet on
the buffalo robe.

"You just shoot 'em," he said.

"But how *cawn* you be sure of striking them? Don't they slither?"

"They slither," Grandfather admitted. "You aim. Aim carefully. You got to shoot 'em in the eye."

After a moment of silence, Miss Margaret, her expression both admiring and incredulous, said, "Oh!" and Grandfather went back to his newspaper.

4

PLUTOCRATS AND HOI POLLOI

❁↯✳↯✦↯✳↯✦↯✳↯✳↯✦↯✳↯✦↯✳↯✳↯✳↯✳↯✳↯✳↯✦↯✦↯✳↯✳↯✦✳

THE SOLID CITIZENS of our town agreed heartily on one subject, no matter how vigorously or profanely they might differ on everything else under the Midwest sun. The majority of these Hoosiers were convinced that whatever the small faults our proud, little Indiana county seat might have, it could boast more really important men and women than any other community of its size anywhere. That size in 1901, when I was ten years old, was forty-five thousand persons.

When it came to naming precisely who these selfless, energetic, forward-looking leaders really were, and spelling out the reasons for the choice, there was a fine difference of opinion; and in support of the differences a combative spirit sometimes asserted itself. The Irish and Germans had their own convictions and voted accordingly. Descendants of the first settlers, the lawyers, doctors, bankers and leading merchants living in the old "homesteads," had other ideas.

The Irish tipped their hats to no man because he lived in a big house, probably inherited from a bloodsucking landlord. How, they demanded, had the town's blasted pioneers ever got so rich, that they could leave great estates and bank accounts to sons and grandsons who voted Republican and wore neckties on weekdays?

The second generation Germans did tip their hats when occasion demanded. Like the Irish, the majority of them voted Democratic and in their "bloody Eighth Ward," precinct politicians made the most of it.

At our house, the names of the original families were sanctified. Did anyone deny that these sturdy settlers had possessed all the sterling qualities set down in the copybooks? Told that people much like our founding fathers had opened western Pennsylvania, Kentucky and Ohio, we shook our heads. We knew better. Our first settlers had been special and unique.

Pistols on hips, wagons stuffed with fine mahogany furniture, boxes of linens and books and an old-fashioned portrait or two, these pioneers had found their hard way over Allegheny trails to Kentucky. There they might remain a year or so, to acclimate themselves and their gentlewomen to wilderness ways; then they turned north across the broad Ohio River to the outpost of Madison, sitting smugly on its high bluff. Then north again they pushed, seeking fertile, well-drained and well-watered flat land at fair prices.

They came individually, an ambitious man and his wife, perhaps a child or two, or at most a handful of families, not in dusty wagon trains like prairie pioneers. The women sat calmly upright on the hard seats, as ladies should, and the men either drove the teams or took their turns out-riding in advance on horseback, precariously exploring the trails that served as roads. Some of them paused at the junction of Fort Wayne's three clean rivers, where a fellow named Barr was making a survey with crude instruments and planning some day to lay out a little town. Others, dreams still unrealized, pushed "farther west."

The freshly painted, well-greased wagons, often with a milk cow or two tethered at the rear, were pulled by stout Belgian or Scottish horses. These families were escaping from neither a sheriff nor starvation. They merely sought elbow room. Few arrived rich, none desperately poor, but before their grandsons were born, many of them had made handsome fortunes, often simply by pausing at the right time and sitting quietly on the right land.

Some of these new acres had been government "reserve," already snatched from the ousted red man when he was bundled off to the West; some had been owned by Miamis, Shawnees or occasional Pottawatomies, who by happy miracles had escaped the exodus. Both the Indians and the Great White Father considered any offer of a dollar an acre for a quarter section of rich soil more than reasonable.

Anglo-Saxon names—Bass, Ewing, Hamilton, Hanna, Holman, Morgan, Williams—joined the French Peltiers and Comparets, Bouries and Centlivres and Avelines, some of whom a half-century earlier had lived within or just outside the log fort in the wilderness. These French had been explorers, fur traders, *coureurs de bois,* or peacemakers between the Indian tribes or between tribes and whites. Some of them remained to help develop the settlement; others roamed on to new forest clearings.

Those who stayed kept far-sighted eyes open, never missing a bet or passing up a good buy or prosperous sale. They traded in flour and molasses, whiskey and gunpowder, ironware china, tobacco and gum boots. Particularly in land, quarter sections at first, then blocks, finally fifty-foot lots.

Some had brought professions with them: surveying, accounting and the law. They started family fortunes in the prosperous, if unfortunately brief, fur trade. They dreamed of a plank road, then a canal, and having accomplished both, they planned a new steam railroad, like those that were picking their way west across Pennsylvania. They "organized" the county as a distinct political entity, and founded the first bank at the same time. They laid out streets, built houses to live in, then mortgaged them to raise funds for a "free school," and hauled in an old hand press to print the first newspaper. They opened a tannery and harness shop, a dry-goods store, brewery and an iron foundry.

We all knew who these early settlers had been, could count their names off on our fingers, tell you approximately when they had arrived, whether or not they had taken improper advantage of the Indians. We could report precisely where their descendants—grandsons and granddaughters—lived; how many red-brick three-story business "blocks," houses large or small, subdivisions, vacant lots and farms an "old family" now owned, or how much Pennsylvania Railroad or Home Telephone stock it kept in the vaults of which local bank.

Ours being a small city, secrets were badly kept and everyone knew, or pretended to know, which of these men, now civic leaders, did or did not overindulge in hard cider or corn liquor. We knew whether they had developed extravagant or reckless tastes, running from imported French wines to "third alarm" applejack, stealthily handmade on a farm near Churubusco or Monroeville. Through leaks at Court House and City Hall, it was even known which members of the current generation had paid their taxes promptly and which poor fellows were dangerously in arrears.

Grandfather Goshorn, engineer and surveyor who did not pretend to be an architect, talked appreciatively of the homesteads the pioneers had built. They had sought flat land with a small rise on which to place the "Big House," as nearly as possible in the center of their acreage. The sites had trailed the skirts of the retreating wilderness and eventually lay near the middle of the growing city.

They built well, Grandfather said, wedding good taste to construction sound enough to last a dozen generations. Only the best oak went into joists and beams; and the trim was smooth, black walnut, cut over in Jasper County and sequestered until it had dried properly. Boards with hand-rubbed satin finish were fastened into three-wing panel doors ten feet tall, or stairways six feet wide with handrails supported by elegant balustrades, curling gracefully to the third floor.

Most of the residences were three stories tall, not counting their high "English basements," where kitchen and breakfast room and storage areas were tucked away, along with great brick coolers for milk and cream. Each house had its library, with shelves to the ceiling—it was just as important a room as the kitchen or the double parlors. Atop the third floor often loomed a square cupola with glass sides, though the need to watch from on high for hostile Indians was long gone. In the rear, angling off behind the porte cochère, was a substantial servants' wing, usually two stories, with at least one fireplace and a big woodbox full of dry oak or maple.

When these mansions were ready to be occupied, it often required a trip for final purchases, usually by canal boat and Great Lakes ship in the days of later pioneers, or a generation earlier, down river in a half-breed's pirogue. The journey might end in Europe, to buy rugs in Brussels, plaster ceiling ornaments and marble fireplace facings in Paris, silk draperies in Lyons, Belfast linens to be handed down to granddaughters.

From Philadelphia these builders brought home busts of Shakespeare, Scott, Goethe and Edgar Allen Poe, to stand on library tables or parlor mantels or long sideboards in the dining room. The busts were large but not oversized; taste dictated. Before long they were importing their gardeners from France, Germany and Belgium, woodlot managers from Scotland or Luxembourg. The grounds, stretching a long quarter mile in all directions around the Big House, were brushed as clean of sticks and weeds as the deer parks on English estates, and the lawns were rolled almost daily, April through September, by hand of course.

The roofs of the old houses particularly interested my Grandfather Goshorn, because as a bridge designer he dealt in stresses and spans. He explained the minute differences between the two styles of French roofs, the Mansard and Gambrel, the latter slightly more elegant and usually finished in gray and lavender slate from a Hoosier quarry. No house was complete without six or eight imported marble fireplaces; one could count how many from the street, Grandfather pointed out, by knowing how to distinguish between single and double flues.

One day he took me to see a house where an ambitious man had started with a bold plan for a Gothic chateau, but gave it up when part way through the job, leaving only two flying buttresses and a single Gothic window.

"The poor fellow wanted to let himself go. Be an American

Louis Fifteenth," Grandfather said. "The Fifteenth was the
Louis who hired Mansard to design a roof. Put it on the palace
of Versailles." He pronounced it in the solid American way,
"Ver-sales." "Poor fellow found it would cost a lot to be a
Hoosier Louis, more than he could scrape up. So he changed
plans. Left a mess."

The men living on these estates that they or their fathers
had created sent their genteel offspring to expensive Eastern
schools and later to British or German universities. With their
wives they annually "took the cure" at Baden-Baden or Aix-les-
Bains, usually pausing on homeward trips for another look at
the Louvre or to bring an extra set of enameled china from
Limoges.

The young ladies read the classics, which in those days
included Sir Walter Scott. They painted landscapes or still
life in oils or watercolors, on canvas or cardboard, never on
china. They played gracefully on pianos carted precariously
into the wilderness, in later days over the Wabash and Erie
Canal. Fiddles were for men—for raffish frontiersmen—but the
violincello was a ladylike instrument.

These successful pioneers handed down their respected
names not only to equally respected progeny scattered
through our telephone directory, but to streets, avenues and
boulevards, creeks, hills and groves. My generation played
choose-up baseball in Swinney Park, named for Colonel Tom
Swinney and occupied in my youth by the Colonel's three
spinster daughters, whom the neighbors called, simply, "the
Swinney girls," the youngest of whom was sixty-five. There at
the west end of Jefferson Street, where the cutter races started
and ended on snowy Sunday afternoons, the house still stands,
an historical museum keeping alive the memory of Colonel
Tom, born in 1803.

McCulloch and Williams Parks both honored early families:
McCulloch was where the workers in Mr. J. J. Woods' electric
motor plant used to sit on the grass, in defiance of all signs,
eating their lunches and talking about organizing a union; and
Williams was where the Dog-and-Pony shows pitched their
disappointingly small tents.

Boys did their lessons in the dingy Rudisill and Hanna schools, or the brighter Hoagland. Whites, Hamiltons and sober, proper Nuttmans lent the probity of their reputations to important banks. Even steam-fire engines were named for Charley Zollinger and Grandfather's friend City Engineer Randall. Zollinger, G.A.R. veteran, sheriff and mayor, was doubly honored by our battery of field artillery that staggered off to the Spanish-American War carrying his name on a banner.

My mother had friends in the homesteads. When I visited them with her, the candlelight impressed me, glowing on walnut and mahogany in the double parlors, where a square-jawed ancestor glowered from a gold frame above one fireplace, and above another a gentle lady with lace on her hair looked out meekly from a less ornate border. Mother preferred the library to any parlor. It was a special delight when Mr. Montgomery Hamilton would push the tall, walnut ladder along its rail and climb rapidly to take a book from a top shelf, fourteen feet above the floor, then appreciating youthful interests, let me climb up to put it back. The libraries all had the same delicious scents: of fine, old leather bindings; a trace of smoke from the coal fire in the grate; kerosene from the student lamp with its high, brass reservoir; and rich tobacco tying all the other smells together.

Preferring the candlelight, I always wondered why our society editors never tired of pointing out that "the spacious edifice was handsomely decked with flowers," with "brilliant illumination from elegant bronze fixtures, hanging below exquisite plaster rosettes in the ceiling."

Such stories in the daily press created unfortunate controversy in the town, my elders said. Talk of "spacious edifices" and "brilliant illumination" made the rebels in Irishtown remember that the owners were blasted rich.

Just who did these people in the big houses think they were? the Irish asked. Had they ever worked? They had no claim to glory just because they were descendants of early settlers. The frontier gentry had not been "special and unique." Granted their offspring had invested loose money in local projects designed primarily to help "the common man," which simply meant "the poor." Granted they organized the gas and electric companies, the real estate additions abutting about-to-be-built roads, and of course the new electric streetcar line. Did that excuse their profits?

These objections bothered some people. But not Mr. John Bass. A Kentuckian who came early to town and became an iron car-wheel impresario and reputedly the richest citizen, Mr. Bass set one of the first examples of sound private enterprise by going personally and alone into the streetcar business. When the local traction company, in laying out its lines, ignored the foundry and machine shop on South Hanna Street, Mr. Bass solved the problem neatly and with dispatch. He built his own car line that wandered two miles through the muddy east-side and south-side neighborhoods where his employees lived, and ended dramatically at the foundry gates.

Thus he not only provided transportation for his loyal working force on days too wet or wintry for bicycles, but sold ticket books at six rides for a quarter. It was a fair price and he made a fair profit. He did not care what anyone said about him. He once even was heard to boast that he had voted for Alton B. Parker for President on the Democratic ticket.

Irishtown, where the most vocal dissenters lived, was a region of small, frame houses, looking across weedy lots at muddy, uncurbed streets. The houses, usually unpainted, with several families sharing a pump and paying rent of three or five dollars a month, often had cracks that needed stuffing, and according to one indiscreet police court judge, the wood fires sometimes were stoked with elm, oak and walnut cut by night from the back forties of the landed gentry.

The district lay, roughly, east and north of good Father Tom O'Leary's handsome new St. Patrick's Church. The whole city was proud of that elegant edifice. Even a few Lutherans, who would not have been caught dead inside, were heard to praise at least its exterior. So no one was surprised when Mr. Tom Toomey returned from a New York meeting of either the G.A.R. or the Knights of Columbus—riding his annual pass as a senior Pennsy Railroad employee—to report that the other

St. Patrick's the whole East Coast was raving about might be slightly larger than Father Tom's, but it definitely was not as beautiful.

The elder generation of the Irish I knew as a boy were sons and daughters of the broad-shouldered men who came over the ocean under sail, to hand-dig the Wabash and Erie Canal. The canal, which would "open up the West," was built before Grandfather Goshorn arrived on the Indiana scene, but it was an "engineering miracle" and he liked to talk about it.

The Canal Company, in a moment of daffy genius, had imported two groups to excavate the big ditch, at an appreciated fifty cents per ten-hour day; first, three hundred good Christians from County Cork, then nearly that many black sinners from Ulster in the Protestant North. Of course, asked-for trouble arrived with them.

At first the factions restricted their religious discussions to Sabbath afternoons along the canal bank, emphasizing fine points of theological divergence with spades, pick mattocks, iron bars, bottles that always seemed to be handy, clubs, and well-aimed dornicks. "A dornick," Grandfather Goshorn always paused to explain, "was a heavable bit of hard rock, the right size to fit a big hand." A man from Cork had told him so.

For a time the contending groups engaged only in private war. Then one dark night some pious fellows stole three muskets, a brace of pistols and three kegs of dynamite from a farmer's wagon.

"That did it," Grandfather said. "The two forces marched on one another on July 11, 1835. Another glorious anniversary of the Battle of the Boyne. You can look that event up yourself."

I did. It was just another Irish-English, Catholic-Protestant row beside an Irish river.

The ensuing mayhem on the new ditch was quickly known throughout the nation as the "Canal War." The Irish meant business, but militia companies appeared surprisingly fast; and the first thing the latter-day crusaders knew, they were digging dirt forty miles apart. The war ended as fast as it began.

The Canal Company imported Germans next, several hundred hearty fellows from Wurttemberg, Bavaria, and the Schwabian *Alb*. These newcomers, instead of warring with one another, spent melodious Sabbath afternoons together, Catholic Bavarians and Schwabian Lutherans, drinking vast quantities of beer and singing endless sad old *Lieder* from *Uns Vaterland*. They composed the backbone of the Eighth Ward, which ran from the tall gates of Mr. Herman Berghoff's handsome Dortmunder Brewery to the Concordia Lutheran Cemetery.

The good burghers spoke in an accent known locally as "Plattdeutsch," which plainly was not the native speech of either Goethe or Schiller. Few of them read Goethe or Schiller for that matter, but all were avid daily consumers of Herr Anselm Fuelber's *Abendpost* and Herr Herman Mackwitz's profitable *Freie Presse-Staats Zeitung*.

These Teutonic Hoosiers were unblushingly proud of the Germany which most of them, like my Grandfather Adam, had fled precipitously on a dark night, rather than suffer the indignity of the goose step. They worked hard and steadily and never filched stovewood from anyone's back forty. They bought their wood honestly for fifty cents a full cord, and they were not above measuring the cord carefully with a foot rule—four by four by eight—before parting with their money.

If cracks should occur in the roofs or walls of their neat homes, they sealed them; and as soon as they could afford it, they built large frame houses for their large families. These they garnished with carpentered Gothic frills, small round towers or bulging bay windows, usually on the second floor, reminding their owners of the houses of the rich folk they had admired across brick walls back home in Stuttgart, Munich or Gmundt. Not that they would have returned to Germany. Here in Indiana no one need step off the sidewalk when an officer went past. Besides, money was easier to make.

They invested carefully hoarded earnings in corner lots and built "business blocks," with fifty feet of frontage on the street, two-story and three-story brick structures for grocer, baker and butcher shops or elegant millinery stores on the first floor, modest living quarters in "railroad flats" above. In the peak of each front, the owner's name was set proudly in deathless stone, along with the year of construction, just as Grandfather Goshorn's name adorned our county bridges. Today, many of the names remain immortalized, and for a Chamber of Commerce that likes things new, the dates are recurring headaches. They reach all the way back to 1871.

These good citizens made sauerkraut, sausage and dandelion wine, scrubbed their front stoops every summer morning, grew vegetables in their back yards and in front old-fashioned flowers in geometric beds; and large, fat cats slept in the sun on their windowsills.

Some bought their sauerkraut in Mr. William Schwier's grocery on Montgomery Street. Mrs. Schwier's kitchen was so clean you could eat off the floor, I heard an admiring *hausfrau* tell my mother; and due to a misunderstanding on my part, for many years I had a charming mental picture of Mr. and Mrs. Schwier, both of ample girth, sitting on the floor eating sauerkraut.

By the time my Grandfather Goshorn explained to me the national origins and inborn customs of our neighbors, second-generation and third-generation Irish and Germans had moved solidly into our retail trade and had found their way, with little trouble, to the public payrolls. All over town the Germans owned respectable saloons that specialized in cool beer and big free lunches. Each advertized, "The largest five-cent glass in town." Other sons of the Rhineland worked as skilled craftsmen, tailors, carpenters and chair caners, many as molders and pattern-makers at John Bass's car-wheel foundry. Naturally they made up most of the skilled labor force at Mr. Berghoff's brewery.

Many Irish were serving as policemen. In enforcing the law, at least, if not in their political views, they were tolerant men; and a fight had to assume the proportions of a monumental fracas before they stepped in to crack heads and make arrests. They had an entrancing habit of just happening to be looking the other way when small boys engaged in such devilment as climbing on the fountain in Mr. Bass's front yard on Berry

Street, or heaving snowballs at Mr. Clem Edgerton, who had no idea of the seasons and insisted on riding his bicycle even through six inches of snow.

Few other "foreigners" came to town in my boyhood. Gradually both Irish and German were assimilated, and now and again the Irish complaints about "first families" were remembered. For some of the offspring of our pioneers did not follow in their forefathers' pious and honorable footsteps, which of course made life more interesting.

Two "scions of distinguished families," the *News* reported one evening, had been arrested for burglary, and one of them unfortunately was shot for his trouble.

When another "prostrated" first family became involved in a startling affair, the same paper's headline was "Love's Freak," with the intriguing subheads "A Terrible Discovery" and "Affianced Bride." The *Journal,* showing admirable restraint, labeled its report of this horrid event with the words "Death Tolls Wedding Bells," saying only that "two prominent young people" were found dead, thanks to a leaky gas line, in the lady's bed chamber.

Miss Jennie Murphy, the laundress, after reading the stories twice, remarked with a sniff, "It goes to prove there's many a sow's ear in them big houses."

My mother's answer was quick and eminently proper. She pointed out that these unhappy, much publicized events were merely the exceptions that proved every good rule. Of course, the rule to which she referred was *noblesse oblige.*

"Noble rank requires honorable conduct," she translated.

5

UNCLE GUSTAVE, MR. CHARLES DARWIN AND CAPTAIN CHARLEY REECE'S BRAVE-BOYS-IN-BLUE

THE FAVORITE uncle of the younger generation in our old red-brick house on Montgomery Street as the nineteenth century was limping to its end was my father's brother Gustave, who liked children, dogs, bluepoint oysters, Japanese art, pretty actresses and Strauss waltzes, and who didn't hate cats. Uncle Gustave leaned his bike against the horse block at the curb one summer afternoon, strolled up the brick walk to the porch for a little chat and remained four or five years.

We children liked him particularly because he had a way of talking man-to-man instead of treating us like simpletons, and he never, absolutely never, stirred juvenile wrath by patting anyone on the head. He also was a free-handed sportsman and philanthropist, who thought nothing of putting out a nickel instead of the usual penny when he found himself in both funds and an over-generous mood.

"Spend it recklessly," he always encouraged us. "Squander all of it!"

Uncle Gustave himself was a bit reckless at times. He smoked Mr. Al Alter's expensive five-cent cigars which, he liked to point out, had genuine Cuban wrappers, instead of the two-for-fives that most gentlemen of our acquaintance bought at Mr. Cooney Bayer's Smoke Shop. An easy-going bachelor, he paid my mother a handsome ten dollars a week for board and room. He also supplied the Thanksgiving turkey and occasional pails of fancy, green ice cream with nuts in it, that he bought at twenty-five cents a quart from Mr. Gus Aurentz, the fashionable ice-cream man who brought the new, exciting word "confections" to our town. Mr. Aurentz had a splendid reputation as the soul of courtesy. He could walk backward rapidly among the little round tables in his establishment, at the same time bowing from the waist to ladies coming in for a ten-cent sarsaparilla ice-cream soda. He even said, "Thank you," to children.

My admirable uncle was an ice skater of grace and elegance who could cut beautiful figure eights on the lake at Reservoir Park; and as a winner of bicycle races, he had garnered a collection of red, white and blue ribbons stamped in gold which he kept pinned to the dimity curtain at his bedroom window. One of these trophies was for winning a "century run," a hundred sweaty miles in one summer day, Fort Wayne to a crossroad northeast of Wabash and back on the Plank Road. He had nosed out the famous champions, Mr. Clem Edgerton and Mr. Larry Randall, who both sold bicycles and presumably had more time to practice.

Bicycle riding was serious business, a test of endurance as well as a sport, and except for a steam locomotive or a runaway horse, it was the fastest mode of transportation. People got to work on bicycles. There were few telephones, so "wheelmen" must deliver messages; even the railroads employed callers to peddle swiftly to the homes of trainmen to notify them that a freight was being made up and when it would leave the roundhouse in the East Yards. Everybody was proud of the "bicycle corps," also known as the "flying squadron," in our sixty-man police department.

Families on bicycles took "constitutionals" together before breakfast, and joined their neighbors in meets, drills, runs and exciting carnivals. My father, who owned a Columbia, belonged to the exclusive Fort Wayne Cycle Club, with fancy headquarters on Calhoun Street; and he told vivid stories of the carnivals, of bunting woven in the spokes of the wheels, streamers fluttering from handlebars and riders carrying transparencies, dressed up as devils, dudes, sailors, knights, jockeys and Indian Chief Little Turtle.

One man's wheel was even covered to look like a racing yacht, with lighted Japanese lanterns swinging from a rack above it. The "ordinaries," with a high front wheel and a little one behind, with a step for mounting and a cord to pull for a brake, were no longer snapping legs and necks by then; and the lower "safeties" had become the rage.

At one banquet at the Wayne Hotel, while my father still was a bachelor, there had been a seven-course dinner, the most elegant served in the city until then, and he had excited the diners with a speech on "The Age of Wheels." The previous year the leader of the parade had been dressed as a Turk, and seventy "wheelers" were ready in line when a horse, jealous probably of the coming of the machine age, delayed the procession. It was hauling the "ammunition wagon," supposed to plant "red fire" flares to light the way, when it suddenly realized that it had had enough of such foolishness and lay down in the street and refused to budge. By the time the driver pulled the horse up and the procession got going, fifteen thousand people lined the route, about a third of the population of the town at the time.

My mother owned a bike, but so far as I remember, she did not ride. Urged, she would answer, "In bloomers? And scare the horses?"

Uncle Gustave always said, "Oh, come, the horses are used to it now."

But he laughed hard, for there had been such an incident once. A farmer's horse, hitched to a buckboard in front of Mr. Ditto's grocery while the driver was inside, had leaped into the air and galloped away when two bold lady riders pedalled by clad in bloomers; and before the animal could be caught he had smashed the rig against one of Mr. Higgins' Pleasant Lake Ice Wagons. The horse undoubtedly was frightened not only by the bloomers, but by the puffed satin sleeves on the ladies' shirtwaists, shaped like balloons.

My mother had other reasons for not riding, I suspect. She

preferred to spend any spare money she might have saved on
books rather than bicycles. The best wheel, at either Mr.
Edgerton's or Mr. Randall's stores, cost a hundred dollars. A
tandem, which Uncle Gustave said he might be able to afford
if only he had someone to ride with him, cost a hundred and
fifty dollars.

Many young people, romantically inclined, did afford them.
One of the stories my mother enjoyed telling was how her
friend Miss Edith Hamilton, famous later as one of America's
truly illustrious Greek scholars, shocked her Grandmother
Pond. The young lady, who at the age of ninety was to be
made at the Acropolis an honorary Citizen of Athens, had come
in breathlessly one Sunday afternoon and announced that she
had just had a delightful hour, riding tandem to the village of
New Haven and back, twelve miles round trip, with that
"charming Mr. Murphy."

"What charming Mr. Murphy?" her mother asked.

"Why, that nice policeman on our beat," Miss Edith replied,
and generations of New England Ponds rolled in their graves.

I remember Officer Murphy. He was tall and thin, with a
big upper lip and pink cheeks and light blue eyes, and once he
gave me a yard-long wire of licorice.

My father still used his bicycle after he was married. But he
never won any ribbons. At least none ever hung on his window
curtains, perhaps because he no longer was a bachelor like
Uncle Gustave.

Summer evenings on the upstairs porch at the house on
Montgomery Street, Uncle Gustave often played his zither for
us, and Sabbath afternoons in his bedroom he would read
from his *Thirty-Volume Appleton's Science Set*. At times,
when something in the set particularly interested him, he
would call us in and translate it into language he thought we
could understand. From my uncle and his handsome set, we
learned, for instance, how the first aborigines were Romans, or
how there were two Stone Ages, the Old and the New, or how
the explorer first pointing the way to the South Pole was an
Englishman. His name was James Clark Ross and would we
try to remember it?

Whether we understood or not, the twins and I liked the sessions in the upstairs front room full of cigar smoke, with the big black canvas sitz bath in a corner. It was a modern sitz bath without a tub of hot water for his feet, I heard him tell Mr. Slentz, who came to clean the wallpaper. We children tried hard to be on hand when Uncle Gustave used the bath. Once in a while we succeeded. Inside the black cube, about four feet square, with the small hole in the top of the canvas buttoned around his neck, he would sit on a wooden stool, sweating splendidly, while an alcohol burner sent up waves of salubrious heat. I realize now it was the forerunner of the gas chamber, and only slightly less deadly.

We enjoyed Uncle Gustave's room also because it was so elegantly cluttered. For whenever money burned holes in his pockets, our wonderful uncle would get out the catalogue of oriental masterpieces from Vantyne's store in New York and send off a money order for some Chinese, Japanese or East Indian knickknack, sight unseen. Punch bowls of twenty-gallon capacity, urns capable of holding the ashes of an entire dynasty, screens, gay paper lanterns, prints, taborets in teak and ebony, temple gongs—if Vantyne's sold it, Uncle Gustave bought it.

My mother was happy with some of the Japanese prints he gave her, and she had them framed. She fancied in particular several landscapes with wind-blown trees, angry clouds and a benign mountain smiling down through squally weather by an artist named Hiroshige. She also permitted the bronze Chinese stork to stand, five feet tall and full of grace, on the living-room hearth. But all else she banished immediately to Uncle Gustave's room, which looked, she told him, like a second-class opium den.

Uncle Gustave didn't mind. He admired my mother, but it was his own life and he enjoyed all of it. For besides collecting oriental splendors, winning bicycle races and playing "Kentucky Babe" and "Bluebell" on his zither, he had a really important job. He was the distinguished young receiving teller, at a princely thirty-five dollars a week, in Mr. John White's National Bank. His name was even on the letterhead, and accord-

ing to Mother's friend Miss Margaret MacPhail, the Bloomingdale school principal, who adored him at a distance, he was
"invaluable" to Mr. White, who would have to shut down the
bank should Uncle Gustave leave him.

Saturday mornings, if I could manage, I used to slip into the
bank by the Wayne Street door, where Uncle Gustave could
not see me. There, for as long as I dared, I would watch rich
people with money in their hands line up in front of his wicket
ready to trust him with their fortunes. How valuable he
actually was to Mr. White I learned one night, when he did
not get home until nine o'clock because the bank's books did
not balance. They probably never would have, if my brave
uncle had not finally insisted recklessly on checking Banker
White's own figures. Thus he discovered that Mr. White had
made ninety-two plus four come to ninety-eight, and to everyone's surprise, instead of being furious Mr. White was actually
grateful. I was proud of this, naturally. In my life simple
addition vied with spelling as the most difficult science
—which it still is.

I cherish particularly one memory of this exciting uncle.
That Saturday afternoon, fortunately or not depending on how
you looked at it, Uncle Gustave was the only adult at home
the day that the Reverend Mr. Wagenhals, the anti-theatre
preacher at Trinity English Lutheran Church, came for a
pastoral call. Uncle Gustave had gone to his room, removed
his pants and hung them over the top of his closet door to
preserve their crease. He was sitting in his long underdrawers,
reading his *Thirty-Volume Appleton's Science Set*, when the
Reverend Mr. Wagenhals got off his bicycle and stood it against
our hitching post.

The Lutheran pastor was a gentleman of unimpeachable
morals, military bearing and rather awesome dignity, with
long, white, curly whiskers that were stained brown around
his mouth, from cigar smoke, my mother explained. He patted
me on the head that afternoon, and I told him that I would
call Uncle Gustave.

Uncle Gustave did not seem exactly jubilant when I announced his caller. He huffed a little as he got into his pants,

and after greeting the minister, who remarked that he had not seen him in church lately, he seemed for once to have very little to say. But what he did say after a time shocked poor Mr. Wagenhals terribly.

"I have been reading my *Thirty-Volume Appleton's Science Set*," Uncle Gustave told him, "about Mr. Darwin's ideas on evolution." Mr. Ernst Haeckel had made these ideas very clear, he said, and they certainly sounded reasonable to any thinking man. "I believe Darwin is absolutely right," he added firmly.

Mr. Wagenhals fell speechless at this blasphemy, a condition to which he rarely descended, and for the rest of the pastoral visit he could only sit very straight in his chair, stroking his curly whiskers and clearing his throat. Finally he mumbled something about another important engagement, staggered to his bicycle and scorched up Montgomery Street at a frightening eight miles an hour.

Having weathered that reckless moment without being struck dead for his impiety, and encouraged by the Reverend Mr. Wagenhals' rare attack of speechlessness, Uncle Gustave decided that it was only proper for him to share his considered views on Mr. Darwin with all his fellow citizens. So he wrote a long letter extolling the dreadful Theory of Evolution to the *Evening News*. He never wrote anything to the *Journal Gazette* or the *Sentinel*; they were Democratic papers and therefore should not be encouraged.

His letter arrived at the *News* on a dull afternoon and so delighted Acting Editor John Dougall that he published it in full and happily awaited reverberations. They came swiftly. Both Herr Professor John Ungemach of St. Paul's Evangelical Missouri Synod German Lutheran School and Catholic Bishop Joseph Rademacher of Immaculate Conception Cathedral replied, using almost identical arguments. Both were doubly shocked, first at Uncle Gustave and next at finding themselves standing firmly side by side in any theological discussion.

Platoons of less illustrious citizens took pen in hand. They joined in dissecting Uncle Gustave and pointing out the godless Mr. Darwin's abysmal ignorance of gospel truth. For more than a week, delighted Editor Dougall printed so many letters that they had to be carried over to page eight. Uncle Gustave hoped that at least one respectable, intelligent person in Fort Wayne would have enough courage and common sense to support him, but so far as letter-writing went, his only defender was Mr. Peg Miller, the town's most outspoken Socialist agitator, who worked for the *Labor Times Herald*.

Uncle Gustave was not exactly an avid reader or supporter of the *Labor Times Herald's* editorials, so he was not highly pleased by Mr. Miller's thundering support. And while Herr Professor Ungemach and Bishop Rademacher were content with one fiery letter each, Mr. Miller persisted with half a dozen additional half-column dissertations defending Uncle Gustave. This, my father said darkly, might cost Uncle Gustave his job at the bank.

Father nervously awaited the news that his younger brother had been fired, finding a little private amusement, meanwhile, in imagining how Pastor Wagenhals must have looked when Uncle Gustave let him have it with both Darwinian barrels. In the end it developed that although Banker White was frightfully shaken, he called in his partners to discuss the problem, and they decided that to fire the receiving teller would only create more bad publicity. So Mr. White just ushered Uncle Gustave into his private office and chided him for his godless irresponsibility and let it go at that. Mr. White explained that he, a bank president, certainly would never tell anyone, employee or stranger, what to think about the Creation; and no one could deny it was very bad judgement for any receiving teller to think aloud in the *Evening News*. The thirty-five dollars a week was safe.

Several years later Uncle Gustave voluntarily left the bank and prepared to go West in search of what he called "a more salubrious climate." He had moved out of our house in the meantime and married Miss Dolly Stevens, the Elocution and Reading Supervisor in Fort Wayne's public schools. We all admired Miss Stevens, even before she became Aunt Dolly. She was a slim, good-looking, dark-eyed young woman with a sense of humor and splendid courage who, season after season, had faced without flinching the daily horrors of her profession. Five days a week, in all weathers, she had pumped her bicycle from school to school, knowing that in every dreary building ambitious teachers were lying in wait with their favorites ready to elocute at her. Always with gestures, of course. Once I heard Aunt Dolly tell my mother that the day had been unbearable. Five times in five different schoolrooms that same horrid little boy had stood on the burning deck.

Dr. Nelson Lloyd Deming was responsible for Uncle Gustave's move West, by warning him to get his cough out of Mr. White's stuffy bank cage and seek some occupation in the open air. Uncle Gustave immediately took off to test the air of Colorado. He had always dreamed of running a cattle ranch but he found no Colorado cattle ranches at bargain prices, so he went on to California. There his search ended in a shabby but ambitious little village called Hollywood, where he bought presumably worthless land that now lies between Sunset and Hollywood Boulevards not far from Vine.

After a few years in which he attempted chicken raising but no cattle, he sold part of this tract to a group of New Yorkers, who had some crazy idea about making moving pictures there. Uncle Gustave reported, in one of his infrequent letters to my father, that their manners were frightful.

Uncle Gustave's own manners were always urbane. After his one Darwinian lapse, he stopped writing to the *News* and gave Banker White no more worries, seeing to it that he dressed, spoke, looked and thought respectably, just as Mr. White wanted him to do. Looking respectable was not difficult. For regardless of what any banker might have wanted, Uncle Gustave's wardrobe, at least, had always been proper. His three-inch collar, starched stiff and sharp as Toledo steel, was ready at all times to decapitate him if he turned his head too quickly without stretching his neck. His watch chain, looped across his vest from his gold watch, looked like a watch chain, not something dragged in from a logging camp; and instead of an elk's tooth, it dangled a medal in honor of Admiral Dewey—not exactly like the one Grandfather Adam wore for a time. This one was real gold.

Uncle Gustave's suspenders were gray with thin, red stripes; and he would just as soon have been caught on the Court House steps without his pants as without a fresh, little flower in his buttonhole in spring and summer. The modest knot in his watered-silk cravat was only the size of a small cabbage, and those were mere chips of diamonds in his horse-shoe stickpin, not expensive-looking enough to make suspicious customers start a run on the bank, nor too flashy for a real gentleman to wear.

Uncle Gustave got along nicely with all kinds of people. The only time I ever saw him really furious was when Miss Belle Clark, society editor of the *Evening Sentinel,* referred to him in print, after the New Year's Cotillion at the Anthony Wayne Club, as "that popular glass of fashion." My parents had gone with him to the dance, the two men in boiled shirts, tail coats and stovepipe hats, my mother in what she always called "my best dress." It was purple velvet, I believe, and amply garnished in furbelows, loops, panniers and frills, and like the men's coats, smelled charmingly of camphor.

Despite his fret at Society Editor Clark, everyone knew that along with Mr. Ernie Rurode, Uncle Gustave shared the title of the best-dressed-man-in-town. Mr. Rurode was owner of the New York Dry Goods Store at Main and Calhoun Streets and was much richer than Uncle Gustave, much older and considerably fatter. He also had an alarming habit of puffing like a Wabash Railroad yard engine whenever he so much as walked rapidly up the aisle of his store. Uncle Gustave never panted.

When Mr. Rurode installed the elevator in his store, it was only the second one in town, the other being the property of Mr. George W. Pixley, haberdasher and president of the new Tri-State Bank. Mr. Pixley's elevator in his four-story office building was a large, square box with plate glass mirrors around the sides, a turkey-red carpet on the floor and over-head an open fretwork through which fascinated passengers could see the big wheels up toward the roof and the inadequate-looking ropes that hoisted the box. It was an unnerving experience.

The elevator in Mr. Rurode's store, on the other hand, was a charming confection of gilded arabesques and cutglass pendants, and it had deeply padded velvet seats along two sides, on which ladies could sit while being yanked upward to the second floor. There, lying in wait, was Mr. Rurode's elegant stock of Gossard corsets at a dollar and five cents, corset covers at twenty-five, petticoats, bustles, long black stockings, muslin nightgowns worth ninety-nine cents, for sale that day at fifty-nine. As the cage rose, the whole building seemed to creak; and arriving at its destination, the contraption came to a shuddering halt and shook itself wildly like a hound dog coming out of the water.

That was fun! But we children would not have traded Uncle Gustave and his room full of oriental splendors and cigar smoke for ten Mr. Rurodes, each with ten elevators.

His position as the city's leading merchant prince gave Mr. Rurode other unfair advantages over Uncle Gustave. Twice a year this rich man took an expensive sleeping car—always insisting on a lower berth, gossip said—to New York City to replenish the stock in his store. He bought acres of ticking, twill, cheviot, honest blue serge, tweed, linen, calico, flannel, cambric, velvet and voile, whole bins of notions, ladies' delicate undermuslins, taffeta petticoats that-rustle-like-genuine-silk, and fine batiste corsets armored and buttressed with real whalebone. He also brought home all the latest decent styles from Paris, France, and clucked knowingly to my mother about what some of the other styles, which he would not touch, were like. As for shirtwaists, he need not spend valuable time seeking them in New York. Wasn't Mr. Sam Foster, one of our most distinguished citizens, known far and wide as "the father of the shirtwaist," because he not only invented it, but made all kinds by the thousands in his factory right here at home?

On his trips to market, Mr. Rurode took time to buy the gray striped pants, gray vests with white piping and smoked pearl buttons, and dark morning coats that everybody admired when he passed the collection plate with such splendid dignity at Pastor Wagenhals' church. On the other hand, Uncle Gustave, who brought his suits off the racks at Mr. Reuben S.

Patterson's latest-styles-for-men-and-boys store, dressed every inch as handsomely as Mr. Rurode and saved his money for Chinese bronzes and Japanese art.

But even with patches on his pants, anyone would have recognized Uncle Gustave instantly as a very important person. Strangers, passing him on Calhoun Street, which was a sort of Hoosier Champs Élysées with an occasional Unter den Linden accent, often turned to look at him admiringly. Here on pleasant summer evenings, he took what he liked to call his "constitutional." Sometimes he invited me to walk with him, and I never refused. Interesting people, and sometimes adventure, crossed our path.

One such pleasant, exciting evening I remember happily, down to many small, bright details. It was April, 1898; I was seven years old, and Captain Charley Reece and his Brave-Boys-in-Blue, members of the glorious if slightly under-drilled Fort Wayne Rifles, were on their way to win the Spanish-American War. The whole town was out, and farmers had come in from all over the county to stand at a little distance in side streets, holding their horses' bridles against the moment a band would begin to play and frighten innocent farm nags out of their senses.

Our mayor, Mr. Henry Scherer, was a patriotic public servant with a wholesome reputation for honesty, integrity and fiscal responsibility. He also was a man of ample waistline who occasionally was known in moments of confusion to make pronouncements while mumbling through his mustache, which was unfortunate, even though it was a handsome mustache that made every papa walrus in the zoo terribly envious.

This day he did not mumble.

Without hesitation or fear of contradiction, he ordered the departure of the Brave-Boys-in-Blue to be marked with "fitting patriotic ceremonies," as they boarded what he called the "troop train." The train consisted of a coach and baggage car hooked to a little locomotive on the Lake Erie and Western Railroad. The Mayor's pronouncement meant that Colonel D. N. Foster, Colonel Robert S. Robertson, Color Sergeants Tom Toomey and Ben Skelton and Judge Sam Hench would

make red-hot patriotic speeches, followed by "remarks" from
less illustrious members of the G.A.R.

Colonel Robertson, who orated every Decoration Day and
Fourth of July, as well as on the birthdays of George Washington, Abraham Lincoln, Generals Ulysses Grant, William Tecumseh Sherman, Phil Sheridan and Mad Anthony Wayne,
was a handsome, trimly bearded man and a thundering old-
school orator. After hearing him, people always said that he
must know what he was talking about. Hadn't he served his
country faithfully in the War against the Rebels? To prove it,
there was the Medal of Honor in plain sight on the lapel of his
dignified frock coat. And after "the war," hadn't he turned his
hand to any civic duty, large or small, with no selfish thought,
from hauling all the poor bankrupts into court for Uncle Sam
to keeping an eye on the weather for everybody? He even had
remained polite and calm that terrible day the dirty Democrats slammed the state senate door in his face and wouldn't
let him into the chamber, in spite of the fact that a lot of good
people had elected him lieutenant governor!

Colonel Robertson could make the stars jump right out of
the flag, but it was Judge Hench who appealed particularly to
me. His speeches were more exciting than the Foster and
Robertson perorations, because the good judge had lost the
lobe of his left ear to a wicked rebel sniper's bullet at the
Battle of Shiloh. His blow-by-blow account of that experience
made any red-blooded boy's hair stand upright—as I remember it, he fell off his horse when the rebel bullet struck. Of all
the oratory I heard in my youth, the speech about Judge
Hench's ear was the best.

Mayor Scherer's "fitting ceremonies" this particular night
included a Mammoth Street Parade with a Mounted Guard of
Honor astride tired horses from Mr. Barnett's bus barn that
usually only pulled the hearse and the hacks. Governor
Mount, who had come all the way from Indianapolis to
participate in this mammoth outpouring of patriotic fervor, led
the cheers. It was a long procession. Members of the Odd
Fellows' Lodge were up toward the front. They walked very
carefully, carrying transparencies, each with a torch inside and

printed on four surfaces proud messages to "Our Brave Boys." Behind them, with American flags and Prussian banners, strode the *Deutscher Waffengenossen Verein,* heroes of the late Franco-Prussian War, who had generously offered their services to President McKinley, only to have him seem indecisive.

Behind the Germans, wearing fancy hats, red and blue suspenders, and carrying nickel-plated axes on their shoulders, the Order of Modern Woodmen marched in two wavering ranks. Then a large contingent of the G.A.R. tramped past singing "Marching through Georgia" as it never has been sung since. In Court House Square, where the old brick county building was being destroyed to make way for one in more suitable granite and marble, patriots had built a gallows and hanged an ugly stuffed dummy, with a placard saying "SPAN-IARD." It was all very exciting, but Uncle Gustave managed to remain calm.

He even seemed slightly amused at young Captain Charley Reece, the first hero-on-his-way-to-war whose hand I ever shook. Captain Charley at the moment was being driven to distraction trying to form his fifty Brave-Boys-in-Blue into files, squads and platoons. The trouble, I heard Uncle Gustave say to the man next to us, was that patriotic but misguided citizens had been setting up free drinks for the heroes at the Court Saloon, down the alley behind the *Sentinel* office, and also in Mr. Boltz' elegant Sample Room below Harmony Hall.

The captain, sweating hard, finally herded his men into a formation of sorts, and they started off to join the impatient Guard of Honor. He kept shouting "hup-hup-hup" as they tried to keep step with the Silver Cornet Band. Mr. Gart Shober's sixteen bandsmen were playing "There'll Be a Hot Time in the Old Town Tonight," and like Captain Reece, Mr. Shober was having a hard time leading them. Mr. Shober had only one arm. He played the cornet with his right hand and with the stump of the left arm kept time.

Poor Captain Reece was bedeviled by other military problems having to do with ordnance and quartermaster items. His sword, dangling at his side, constantly tried to trip him, and he had to hitch it up at every other step. Besides this unhappy situation, many of his Boys-in-Blue actually were in brown, black, gray or checks and stripes, for the uniforms, requisitioned weeks earlier from the state quartermaster general, had not arrived and Captain Reece wanted to know repeatedly, in a loud voice, how President McKinley expected seventy-five thousand new volunteers to win the war without uniforms. It was bad enough to be short of rifles and have no ammunition whatever.

Adjutant Tom Toomey of Sion S. Bass Post of the G.A.R. was holding aloft his old battle flag with its bullet holes from bloody Antietam. He had carried this same flag all through the War of the Rebellion and no other member of the G.A.R., and certainly no mere civilian, dared touch it. Ben Skelton, who lived for the Grand Army and the Republican party and such minor paying jobs as they afforded, carried the post colors to the left of the battle flag. As the flags went by, Uncle Gustave shouted "Hats off!" and jerked off his own boater and stood very still, looking handsome and patriotic. As I glanced up at him, my own cap in hand, I regretted deeply that such a brave man must stay at home, instead of marching away to fight the Haughty-Dons-of-Spain, which I thought was a single word, like Dirty-Rebel.

My mother explained next day that Uncle Gustave was too old to go to war; he was about thirty, while the Fort Wayne Rifles averaged only eighteen and a half. Besides, she pointed out logically, he sunburned very easily. But that night at the Street Parade, I remained disconsolate, realizing that Uncle Gustave, exciting letter writer that he was, would never write home from Chickamauga Park to the newspapers, the way Stinky Eggleston's Uncle Pete was doing.

We did not follow the march to the station, to see all the families crying, but Uncle Gustave heard next day at the bank what had happened. Colonel Foster, Colonel Robertson and Judge Hench, not to mention the less important members of the G.A.R., got very angry with Governor Mount because the heartless creature used up all the speaking time. He never stopped telling how much he loved the Boys-in-Blue until the car wheels began to turn, leaving the two colonels and the judge standing on the station platform, choked with unuttered oratory.

Uncle Gustave, who did not have too high a regard for most politicians, considered this very funny, and all through supper he burst out laughing, thinking of it. He said that the three muzzled men had been suffering oratorical indigestion all night and certainly would make up for the Governor's treatment the next time they found an audience or stepped up to a ballot box.

6

UNCLE GUSTAVE AND THE PERILOUS INVENTION OF MR. ALEXANDER GRAHAM BELL

❀✿❀✿❀✿❀✿❀✿❀✿❀✿❀✿❀✿❀✿❀

E VEN WITHOUT a parade to excite us, we youngsters liked to
stroll up Calhoun Street at any day or evening hour with
our handsome Uncle Gustave and his jaunty walking stick.
Traveling salesmen in the staunch oak chairs on the sidewalk
in front of the Aveline House didn't always glance up, but the
young ladies, who would rather get the binding on their skirts
soiled all around the bottom than ever sit in the Aveline House
chairs, often looked three times. When they did, Uncle Gustave blushed slightly and lifted his hat politely, then quickly
and properly turned his gaze straight ahead.

Uncle Gustave not only was famous for the courtly way he
tipped his hat, particularly to old ladies, but also for the
elegance of the row of hats on the pegs in his closet, each
ready for some special social, patriotic or business occasion. In
summer he usually made do with a straw boater, with the
colors of the St. Joe River Boat Club in its ribbon and bow,
even though he didn't own a boat.

Spring and fall it was a fawn or pearl-gray derby with a
tightly curled brim that his adoring Miss MacPhail, who knew
all kinds of funny words, said was "simply de rigueur." In
winter and at funerals, the derby naturally was black. For
special evening events, he had a gorgeous silk topper, and for

scorching on his bicycle, a tight linen cap with a long visor to keep dust and sun out of his eyes.

On our Calhoun Street walks we liked the pleasant way our uncle greeted his male friends, raising the walking stick in a sort of semi-military salute as if it were a saber. Chiefly we adored his kindly habit of introducing us to interesting and very important people. How else would I ever have met our great reform mayor, Mr. Chauncey Oakley—or Mr. E. B. Kunkle, who owned one of the first, if not the first, horseless carriages in town? Mr. Kunkle ran a small machine shop, and he smelled pleasantly of hot engine oil and wore an impressive mustache, which I once heard my mother tell my father was "obviously dyed."

Had it not been for Uncle Gustave, I would have grown to manhood and tottered to my grave without ever having met Joe-the-Lion-Tamer. Joe, whose real name was Mr. Joseph Griffith, was a thoroughly batty citizen who had come to town with Mr. Barnum's grand two-ring circus and had never left. He claimed to have been Mr. Barnum's chief lion handler, and he spent a haunted life in our quiet town, training imaginary lions and chasing them through the streets when they escaped. For a living, he blacked boots.

My mother, after a serious discussion that I could not understand with Dr. Nelson Lloyd Deming, warned all the men in our house never again to let Joe shine their shoes.

"I distinctly saw him spit into the blacking box to moisten it," she said. "And I don't want you to drag any of his germs in on my carpets."

When I proudly reported that Uncle Gustave had introduced me to Joe, my mother became very angry, not at me, but at my uncle. She reminded him sharply that it was dangerous even to touch "that poor man," and she made me wash my hands with good strong laundry soap.

There also was a happy Sunday afternoon when Uncle Gustave and I were passing Mr. August Bruder's jewelry store and he stopped to chat with the gorgeous Miss Nellie Van Valkenburgh, the famous actress, home briefly from a triumph in New York City's brilliantly gas-lit Herald Square. She was carrying roses when Uncle Gustave and I met her, and she gave me one. This naturally generated a flaming love affair—unilateral, of course—that persisted until the enchanted evening when my good uncle introduced me to Miss Julia Taylor.

Fort Wayne's own Miss Taylor was playing a one-night stand at Mr. Frank Stouder's Temple Theatre in Mr. Charles Major's Hoosier masterpiece, *Alice of Old Vincennes*. She explained in a fine, musical voice that she had been very badly treated in New York by a terrible man named David Belasco and a pair of brothers named Frohman. I immediately declared war on all Frohmans and all Belascos, and looked forward to the day when I could go to New York and take it out in their blood.

Uncle Gustave was a man who blushed easily, and I remember how he flushed crimson, at the same time looking immensely pleased, when the exquisite Miss Taylor, recognizing him fifty feet away in front of Mr. August Bruder's jewelry store, rushed up to him, flung herself into his arms and kissed him. Everybody was watching, too.

My mother explained that people did that sort of thing in New York City, and nobody minded it. For years I had a mental picture of the metropolis, and of Herald Square in particular, with beautiful actresses rushing up to handsome men like Uncle Gustave all over the place and kissing them, while no one paid the slightest attention. Miss Taylor not only was beautiful, affectionate and kind, but she was the first young lady I ever saw wearing mascara. I liked it.

Uncle Gustave certainly liked her, too, I figured. Why else would he have a supper party for her in the Aveline House at eleven o'clock at night, after the theatre, where they ate bluepoint oysters and Welsh rabbit and drank champagne, just the way Grandfather Adam always hinted stage women did?

Uncle Gustave also made me acquainted with Mr. Lee Ivens, the handsome gentleman who presided at the cigar counter in the lobby of the Aveline House, with several of his boxes of cigars under the glass plainly marked "10¢ Each." It was rumored that rich traveling men actually bought them

occasionally and set fire to them. Atop the case, Mr. Ivens
spread a piece of green cloth on which he rolled dice with
local sports and with strangers from Chicago who were willing
to try their luck. They usually regretted it.

Next to Mr. Louie Heilbroner, the distinguished editor of
the *Baseball Blue Book,* Mr. Ivens knew more about many
important matters than anyone else in town, and kept many
arguments from becoming bloody. Mr. Heilbroner never
argued; he just said, "Read it in the *Blue Book,*" and let it go
at that. He was a famous man with a pocketful of tickets for
Mr. Fred Clarke's Pittsburgh ball players and Mr. Clark
Griffith's Chicago White Stockings.

Mr. Ivens didn't tell anyone to look up anything in anything.
He had the answers in his head and no one ever proved him
wrong. His fascinating knowledge included not only the an-
nual batting averages of Mr. Christy Mathewson, Mr. Honus
Wagner and Mr. Nap Lajoie, but how many rounds it took
Mr. James J. Corbett to beat Mr. John L. Sullivan in New
Orleans last September.

Uncle Gustave patiently explained to me that Mr. Ivens was
a great student who had devoted most of his life to gathering
important information, and that people came from miles
around for him to settle their disagreements. He never
charged them for his services, Uncle Gustave said, but the
men who won the discussions usually bought boxes of cigars
and passed them out recklessly.

Uncle Gustave liked good arguments for their own sake,
provided they were conducted without shouting, because, he
said, they kept the mind open and alert. He liked them
particularly at Sunday breakfasts, which in our house were
slow, ample and starchy. These were domestic rituals, conducted comfortably with fresh white tablecloths and fresh
napkins to tuck into shirt collars.

Even my father, a man impatient with any kind of delay or
idleness, consented to wait on the Sabbath until the ungodly
hour of eight for his breakfast. This was partly because we
always had waffles, along with our daily oatmeal, hot coffee
cake and cinnamon cookies.

Miss Amelia Rose, our magnificent maid-of-all-work, earned her three dollars a week and keep on a seven-day basis, and Sunday mornings she could handle two cast-iron waffle makers going full blast on the gas range, flipping them over by hand as fast as we could empty them. My father liked pure maple syrup on his waffles. My mother, who was born in Pennsylvania near the Maryland line, liked chicken gravy, and Uncle Gustave on occasion used both, blending them expertly.

After the dishes were cleared away and my father had hurried off to get ready for church, Uncle Gustave would light his cigar, puff hard at it and discuss grave and urgent matters. This meant that he argued politics with my mother, who believed in Votes for Women and kept herself informed enough to cast a ballot the moment that happy hour arrived. She never bothered to argue with Uncle Martin or another of my father's brothers, Fred, the Lutheran who preached in German; either of them, she said, would vote for Judas Iscariot or John Wilkes Booth were they to run as Republicans.

Uncle Gustave was a Republican, too, but he never would have voted for either Judas or Mr. Booth, even though he sometimes led one to believe that he had been almost single-handedly responsible for the election of Mr. McKinley, and usually referred to Mr. McKinley as "Our Peerless Leader." My mother happened to favor Mr. Bryan and was only mildly impressed by Mr. McKinley's sterling qualities. So every Sunday at breakfast Uncle Gustave went to great pains to convert her to the true American faith.

Like Grandfather Adam, he insisted darkly that Mr. Bryan was "dangerous," a radical who hearkened to the Populists or the Molly McGuires and who never could be trusted not to come out in support of labor unions. It was rumored that Mr. Bryan actually had talked in public once with Mr. Eugene Debs, that crazy railroader from Terre Haute, who had gotten so involved in the railway strike that he went to jail and who, Uncle Gustave darkly predicted, would run for President some awful day. I don't know how Uncle Gustave knew, but I always remembered his prediction each of the four times Mr. Debs did run.

Usually my mother replied to such charges with the flat statement, "Gustave, you sometimes sound as stupid as Martin!"

Uncle Martin, as I may have pointed out before, was not the family's intellectual star. It was he who had stocked the plaster busts of Martin Luther in his drug store, and for years he went trembling about town whispering that the Catholics had buried arms and ammunition under the altar of the Cathedral of the Immaculate Conception. The reason for this cache of armaments, Uncle Martin had on good authority, was to overthrow the rightful government and place the Pope in the White House.

Even I knew better than that, and so did Mr. Berghorn, our friendly milkman, whose unbiased opinion in the matter I asked point blank one pleasant morning. Mr. Berghorn was so startled that he spilled the milk he was ladling out of a ten-gallon milk can without a lid into the glass pitchers our Amelia carried to the curb whenever she heard the milkman's bell coming around the corner. We got two gallons a day, plus cream, and it took time and a steady hand to dip it all from the cans.

Mr. Berghorn did slop the milk over the edge of Amelia's pitcher when I asked the question, and he stared at me with his eyes propped open. "Under the altar?" he repeated. Then he shook his head and mumbled something about it sounding sort of silly to him.

I had believed that Uncle Martin was mistaken as he was about so many things, because all that was buried under the Cathedral altar was Bishop Joseph Dwenger, who died when I was a year old. I naturally had not attended the funeral, but I had heard about it so often that I began to believe I had been there.

Of course, Uncle Gustave did not think like Uncle Martin. No one did. This druggist uncle had the most illogical collection of solid concrete prejudices in our town. But sometimes Uncle Gustave did argue like him. This often was when my mother had broken down his unsound dialectics and he was reaching desperately for rebuttals.

Usually he would sit with his back stiff, steadfastly repeating his patriotic all-American convictions, stirring the cigar ashes in his coffee cup. He always knew that eventually he would lose the argument to my mother, no matter what the subject. He argued with her and lost on politics, religion, whether or not Mr. Hearst sank the battleship *Maine*, whether skirts should be a little shorter so that a woman could skate without tripping herself, whether Machinist Bill Hosey of the Pennsy Railroad shops would make a good mayor.

There was one period of several months when our Sabbath breakfasts were lively with debate about our projected telephone. My father had installed one of the town's first telephones in his drug store in 1889, before he mortgaged the store and lost it when he ran for county clerk. There was no doubt on his part about the need for a telephone in the house, but which one?

By this time Fort Wayne had two telephone companies, the Bell and the Home, fighting each other for business. My mother leaned toward the Bell system, which was said to operate in Chicago and other cities; she was convinced it was here to stay. My father was a violent partisan of the Home phone, chiefly because it had been started by local men, people like Will Vesey, Will Moellering, Sam Foster and Charley Bash, whom, he pointed out, you could trust.

Uncle Gustave wanted neither. A man's courage can go just so far. He had fearlessly defended Mr. Charles Darwin and upset Banker White, but he balked at certain lethal instruments, the telephone among them.

"Everybody knows that telephones attract lightning," he would assert darkly and dogmatically. "It follows the wires into houses and kills innocent people. Think of the children!" he would add, thinking of himself, too.

Uncle Gustave knew the ghastly hazards of both Bell and Home systems, and as far as he was concerned, it didn't really matter whether they were owned in Fort Wayne or Timbuktu. To prove it, he would clip frightening items from the *Evening News* about perfectly sound persons who had been stunned or even killed when lightning leaped out of telephones at them.

"That's strange," my mother would say. "I didn't read about it in my *Sentinel*."

My mother subscribed to the *Sentinel* to be delivered at the house for six cents a week, partly because it admired Mr. Bryan as much as she did, even though its admiration was not based on Free Silver as my mother's was, but because the young man with the golden voice abhorred the demon rum. Uncle Gustave, on the other hand, had been an enthusiastic supporter of the *News* even before it published his letter about Mr. Darwin. So to keep abreast of the unsullied truth, he had to spend a penny for it each afternoon and bring it home under his arm.

I don't remember how many months the telephone argument lasted, but we did get one in the end and it was installed in the upstairs hall. It was a Home phone, my father having registered one of his rare triumphs, and I was happy about the choice, for the Home phone was much handsomer than the Bell. Both instruments were the approximate shape and size of small coffins and each had a mouthpiece sticking out at the end of a long iron arm, like a gun pointed at anyone who used it. But Bell phones were built of dull, black polished walnut, whereas Home phones were gay, varnished quarter-sawed oak.

Uncle Gustave arrived from the bank a few minutes early the day the telephone was put in, and he found the house in a welter of excitement. He went upstairs to look at the lethal instrument and came down at once, very black of face.

"You've put the thing between my room and the bath," he charged. "Right where I have to pass it within three feet."

"Well?" my mother answered.

It was true. The upstairs hall was long and very narrow and the new telephone was hung on the east wall about halfway back. The bathroom was at the rear and Uncle Gustave, quite properly, had the best front room over the parlor.

"A telephone should be downstairs," he said firmly. "In the pantry, if at all. What am I to do when there's a thunderstorm?"

"We put it where we can call Dr. Porter when we need him

in the night, without having to run downstairs," my father
answered.

"And where we can call the police, in case we hear burglars
at the silver drawer in the dining room," my mother added.

That sounded exciting enough. Only as time went on, we
never had to use the telephone to summon Dr. Porter in the
night and there never were burglars. The only thing that did
happen of any interest, and it was so regular that we got used
to it, was the early morning call. This came each day shortly
before eight o'clock when the bell jangled for all it was worth
and someone hurried to answer and the operator would say
pleasantly, "Morning test."

By checking this way, the company could be sure all its
wires were working, so it could give the kind of wonderful
service to its patrons that it advertised. The wires usually
stayed up, except in bad weather. Only when talking to people
who lived away off at the other end of town did we even have
to holler very loud.

Then one morning, after the telephone had been in for
perhaps a month, I was wakened by peals of thunder and
flashes of lightning and Uncle Gustave's voice. When I
reached the hall he was standing in his doorway, dressed only
in his pants and holding a towel in front of his naked chest. He
was telling my mother that a person's life wasn't safe in this
house on such a day, and he was glad he would be at the
bank, and not to expect him home for supper if this weather
kept up.

Mother was busy. So she just told Uncle Gustave not to act
ridiculous, and she went on into the bedroom to dress the
twins. Uncle Gustave finally took his razor, shaving mug,
strop, towel, witch hazel bottle and courage in his hands, and
wearing his pants and the air of a martyr, inched down the
hall toward the bathroom.

I was on the top step, starting downstairs to see what
Amelia had in mind for breakfast, when it happened. Uncle
Gustave had gone as far as the telephone, squeezing past it
against the opposite wall to get through the danger zone,
when there came a tremendous explosion.

The little quarter-sawed oak front door of the phone burst open, the bells shrilled and out of the mouthpiece, like a shell from one of Admiral Dewey's four-inch cannon, a flash of electricity hurled itself at Uncle Gustave's naked chest, just as he had always known it would. Shaving mug, brush, razor, strop, witch hazel flew out of his hands. He had a pleasant tenor voice, never loud, but every man at some time in his life can count on one instant of supreme power. This was his instant.

Joshua tootling at Jericho, I am sure, must have sounded like a tin whistle compared with Uncle Gustave's ringing blast that awful morning. It shamed mere thunder. There he stood against the wall, arms outstretched as if the lightning bolt had pinned him there. The towel fluttered down from around his shoulders and slowly his knees buckled; he made a small choking sound and slid to the floor.

Mother reached him first.

"He's breathing!" she said.

He was more than breathing. He was making strange noises and his eyes were rolling. His mustache drooped. With Amelia's help, Mother dragged him back to his bedroom and there shortly I heard him trying to talk. His voice grew slowly but steadily louder. At last he began to swear. I was listening, fascinated, when my mother grabbed me and rushed me downstairs to breakfast.

After half an hour Uncle Gustave arrived at the breakfast table. He ate as usual, except for feeling his neck, wriggling his head, poking himself here and there with one finger. At last, full of affronted dignity, he picked up his walking stick and took off for the bank.

Of course the day became a landmark. Such-and-such happened "before Uncle Gustave was struck by lightning," or "after Uncle Gustave got hit." But the fact that he had undergone the terror and lived to tell of it did something for him. When the days were clear and there was no cloud in sight, he used to say confidently that lightning never struck twice in the same place. But if there was a storm, he lost faith in that comforting theory without even a blush, and one cloudy morning with murmurs of thunder in the distance, I even remember seeing him duck down to his hands and knees and crawl rapidly past the telephone.

Conversion came finally, as sometimes happens with bachelors who wear flowers in their buttonholes and diamonds in their cravats and introduce small boys to beautiful actresses with arms full of roses. It was perhaps a year later when he remarked at the Sunday breakfast table that it was devilish inconvenient to have only the Home phone in the house. He missed so many calls. The White National Bank had the Bell and so did many of his friends.

"I think, if you agree," he told my mother, "that I'll have a Bell phone put in, too. It will be in my name and I'll pay for it. Is that all right?"

"Of course," my mother said, glancing at my father.

"We can hang it in the pantry," Uncle Gustave went on, "one phone upstairs, one down." He put his flower in his buttonhole, gave the end of his elegant mustache another tight twist, picked up his walking stick and waited for a final word.

"The world do move," Mother said.

"A great age," Uncle Gustave agreed, and started for the bank.

"Is it a great age?" I asked my father.

"Full of seven wonders," he replied.

7

DER KLEINE
KATECHISMUS

M Y FAMILY, when I reached the age of six, bought me a new pair of knee pants, scrubbed my face and hands, combed my hair, gave me a serious lecture on schoolroom morality and forced me, kicking and screaming, into new shoes and long, black stockings. The shoes were high, uncomfortable to feet that had been bare all summer, and the shoe laces, as laces always did, kept coming out of their neat tuck-in at the top. They were out, dangling, and one stocking sagged by the time my father, as unwilling as I myself, walked me to the door of St. Paul's Missouri Synod German Lutheran School and delivered me to Herr Professor Ungemach, the principal.

I remember the details. I had kicked and screamed because of antipathy to wearing shoes and stockings in the warm month of September anywhere at any time. I was not opposed to education. I already knew how to read, my first adventure with a book having been one by Naturalist John Burroughs. Its first sentence on the first page was simple, to the point and at least mildly interesting. "A mouse sat on my hand." All six words were in tall, clear Primer type and the pen-and-ink drawing depicting the event took up half the page. My mother encouraged anyone to read, and her father approved particu-

larly of anyone reading John Burroughs. He had met the
illustrious naturalist in the West, referred to him always as
"my friend" and was glad to buy all the other juvenile works
of this master as they appeared.

I had graduated swiftly from mice and nature to the more
stirring literature of the daily press, and had also had a
pleasant experience with education in our back yard. This was
in the Art School in the original Hamilton carriage house fifty
feet from our dining-room porch. Its big carriage doors faced
north and had needed merely to be fitted with broad window
sashes to afford the proper light. There, since Miss Hollensle-
ben, the teacher, was a tolerant young woman, I had my own
easel, paints and charcoal, and amused myself or was a frightful
nuisance, probably both.

Also, the previous year I had spent several winter months at
a private kindergarten that had unintentionally prepared me
for anything. It was operated in a basement on Harrison Street
by a lady who could not understand my aversion to cutting
tissue paper into silly shapes. There were perhaps a dozen of
us and when we were through with the tissue paper, we
marched around and around the small room while the lady
played the piano. We were not going anywhere, and I never
could get the point of all the unnecessary exercise. I had to
walk beside a little girl named Linda McKinney, who disliked
me as much as I disliked her. Real school, I hoped, would be
better. At least it would be different.

It was. Some of the things that happened to me were most
unusual. St. Paul's parochial *Schule* was a tired, old, dusty
building with widening cracks in brick walls that once had
been red, but several generations earlier had turned mouse
brown. Small boys had further improved the exterior by
writing dirty words in chalk over the smoother surfaces. I did
not realize at the time that the words were dirty; they all were
in German.

The plumbing in this institution of learning was concentrated in two redolent brick structures, open to the weather, at
the far end of what was intended as a play yard; but only the
most reckless youngster dared play in it. It supported not a

blade of grass or even a weed, and just enough sharp, crushed stone had been spread across the well-trampled earth to guarantee bloody knees after every fall.

St. Paul's Lutheran lay only a short block down Barr Street from our house, behind its iron picket fence and double row of elms. This was one of its advantages, since the nearest public school was eight long blocks away. This school had been named in honor of Henry Clay and seemed to embody many of that unhappy warrior's gloomier ideas.

Not that this public school was segregated as to color as Mr. Clay would have desired, with "colored" and "white" signs over the entrances. But there was a sharp division, nevertheless. The door on the east side was clearly marked "Boys," that on the west "Girls." Someone, however, in a frugal or indifferent moment had neglected to build a walk to the girls' entrance. So had that door been used, the rich turf around it would have been trampled. Consequently, boys and girls alike entered from the east, the girls' door was kept locked, and everybody hoped there never would be a panic.

But neither safety nor Christian doctrine, local geography nor the horrendous architecture of the new Clay School influenced my parents' decision in favor of the Missouri Synod. It was languages.

My mother believed in starting modern languages in the first grade and made a nuisance of herself at meetings of the school board plugging her idea. A few years later she even ran for a place on the board, but the city council, which made the appointments, proved its solid Americanism and fiscal sanity by voting her down.

A foreign language was available at St. Paul's Parochial. It happened to be German, but even that was better, my mother thought, than no language at all.

My father was highly dubious of her choice. Even after she pointed out patiently that both Heine and Schiller had written some fine poetry in German, he still objected. His complaint was not with the guttural sounds of the German language as spoken in Fort Wayne. That, he insisted, had nothing to do with it. He was a Lutheran, naturally, but he belonged to the

United wing of that denomination, the Reverend Mr. Wagen-hals' church, which unfortunately never had a school. The Missouri Synod, which Grandfather Adam had helped establish, and the United branch were not on speaking terms at that time; and so in the eyes of the Missouri members, Father was a back-slider, nearly as good a candidate for the Everlasting Bonfire as if he had embraced the godless Church of Rome.

"I'm against the whole damned Missouri Synod and every-thing in it, including Pastor Miller, Pastor Lange and Professor Ungemach," he shouted so loudly one summer day with the windows all open that my mother shushed him. But as usual, he came out second best in this debate.

The town's public schools, in which my mother had taught briefly as a young woman, avoided all costly frills in the elementary grades. In that Cleveland-McKinley era, the Three R's were sufficient and relatively inexpensive. True, if high-school students wished, they could stagger after Caesar across all of Gaul's three parts, and a few hand-picked specimens could even absorb rudimentary Greek.

But what good would such fol-de-rol be for the average boy hunting a job in the Wabash Railroad switchyards or the White Fruit House? The cost of education was frightfully high as it was. In selecting the school board, the city council acted on a basis of staunch party regularity, although it was con-sidered preferable for the members to read and write. Demo-crats usually won, and being the party of frugality, kept grade-school teachers' salaries in the range of seventy-five to one hundred dollars a month.

Problems of conflicting creeds were not exactly new in my family. My parents never argued them, but relatives and relatives-of-relatives liked to bring up the subject, and both my father and my mother as a rule kept their convictions to themselves when there was company present. My mother, born a Presbyterian, had spent her first four school years in a convent—a distressing fact that naturally had reached the keen ears of the teachers at St. Paul's. The cold-water convic-tions of her Scottish Covenant ancestors and the gentle piety of the nuns never really blended in her veins. So she had evolved a pleasant sort of religion all her own; help the help-less, be kind to animals, preserve beauty, promote democracy, read good books, cherish friendships, be hospitable with meals and beds and never, never suffer fools gladly.

She did not go to church except on New Year's Eve at the Cathedral, early Christmas morning at St. Paul's Lutheran, and years later to memorial services for the dead of World War I. She was gracious, if totally unconvinced, toward all proselytizing believers of whatever faith, including Missouri Synod Lutheran and that new creed rapturously embraced by her friends Mr. and Mrs. Tom Ellison, who were Fort Wayne's first blue-ribbon, no-holds-barred Christian Scientists.

At St. Paul's, my mother said, instruction in the Teutonic tongue would not be in the purest Hanovarian accents, but it should provide at least a working knowledge of the language, were it ever needed.

She didn't know the half.

For not only was I the only pupil in Herr Professor Strieter's dingy first-grade room who did not understand a word of German—my only experience with it had been my Grand-father Adam's cozy conversation with his Creator before and after meals—but I also was the only one who came from a home in which it was not the basic language. That being the case, no effort was made to teach German; instead, English, in horrendous Mittel-Europa diphthongs, claimed the most seri-ous attention. And, naturally, all instruction, direction, disci-pline and prayers were conducted *auf Deutsch,* which put me at a distinct disadvantage.

Herr Professor Strieter was the only member of the seven-man, no-woman faculty with whom in three years I came into classroom contact, who might be loosely described as gentle. For example, he always struck his six-year-old charges lightly, with a ruler or his open hand, instead of laying on soundly with a broad wooden paddle or a pink rod with a flexible steel core. It must also be said in his defense that he never hit them at all unless he had been unduly provoked.

I provoked him. I was a *dummkopf* who couldn't under-stand plain, honest German and I was forever doing and saying the wrong things. I even had the atrocious judgment to argue with him once that there was no such English word as "undercoat," after he had explained that we had "undercoats *und* overcoats." He corrected me with the ruler, three sharp whacks, and from then on watched me more attentively.

"The right hand, not left!" he insisted whenever I picked up a pencil. "The right, the right!"

This confounded me. For just that summer in the Hamilton carriage house Miss Norah, one of the artists in the Hamilton family, had warned me, "Don't let anybody make you draw with your right hand. Remind them that Michaelangelo was left-handed and he was rather good."

"Michaelangelo . . ." I tried to tell Herr Professor Strieter. "Who?"

It was no use. I gave up. He didn't understand me any more than I understood him.

My father was half German by inheritance and could speak the language after a fashion, but he always seemed embarrassed when a hearty Teutonic friend addressed him in it and expected a reply in kind. Singing was a different matter.

Sabbath evenings in our house on Clinton Street, he took melodious command. For ninety dollars, which was nearly three weeks' salary, he had bought an oversized, rosewood "square grand" piano from the *Sängerbund Halle*. He had heard it often at concerts accompanying hearty male choruses, and had become enamored of its tone. Nearly forty years later, I saw Mr. John Philip Sousa sit down at it in my own living room, run his fingers over the keys and turn, smiling, to say, "Good! This instrument has guts."

Those Sunday nights my father would strike a few husky chords, and with his children and any visitors supporting as best they could, he would plunge into "Ein' Feste Burg," singing it with conviction. I hear it even now, pushing out the walls. It is understatement to say that he had a hearty voice, and he put it, and something besides, into the German words. Perhaps it was reverence. He sang it the way Martin Luther intended.

Other times he would hum, trying to find a tune, then from

some hidden recess come up with a "stein song" he had not thought of since he was a young man. Except for these evenings, I never heard him use a German word at home.

He did wear a mustache, resembling to that extent the teachers at St. Paul's *Schule*, and it was almost as impressive as theirs, but he never indulged in an oversized beard. Except for Herr Professor Feiertag, our neighbor, and Herr Professor Schroeder in sixth grade, no one in school was smooth shaven. The third-grade teacher, Herr Professor Gerberding, had the most dramatic whiskers by far. They were long, curly and a bit unruly, split in the middle and flowing downward and outward in two graying cascades. Between them, supported by his ample chest, hung a two-foot cherrywood pipe stem with a porcelain bowl at the end. The bowl was six inches tall, gaily painted with birds and flowers and a German motto that no one ever translated for me, topped by a gold filigreed lid. He naturally was proud of it.

Throughout the school day, from eight-thirty in the morning until four in the afternoon, this pipe sent up immense clouds of sweet smoke that made the room, when it was opened unaired each morning for class, smell like the Elks Lodge after the brothers had spent a busy evening in the card room. The good Herr Professor took the pipe from his lips only long enough to speak, spit or spank, or to play his fine imported accordion, not only to lead us in song but any other time the spirit moved him.

He did not compare as a musician with Herr Professor Feiertag. A quiet, smallish man who suffered atrociously, I learned, at the hands of overgrown fifth graders, Herr Professor Feiertag played his violin in class and played it well. At home he organized his wife and three children, who were our friends, into a family orchestra that was in great demand.

No reason comes to mind why I never told my family that almost daily I was the victim of my own stupidity, followed by chastisement. It just did not occur to me. So far as I knew everybody who went to school anywhere got paddled regularly, and why make a fuss? I was too awed and terrified—and slow, no argument. Even I realized at length that it was not being particularly bright to spend the better part of a week grasping how to say "yes" and "no" and "thank you" and "please." It was quicker, I finally discovered, to learn the sounds of the words and not bother with their meanings, particularly in what could be called religious instruction.

Each morning the school day opened with singsong recitations from *Der Kleine Katechismus*. We had to learn it, all of it, word by grim word, beginning to end. And whenever a young sinner missed a line or even a word, he was upended over a desk and had good Christian ethics applied where they hurt most. As I look back, I am sure that the little theology I have been able to absorb in life came to me by way of the seat of my pants.

The day ended at four o'clock, and promptly we stood at our desks and shouted a prayer in chorus. It began, in German of course, "Now we go forth from school and will remain with Thy Word." With the "Amen" and a quick, shouted "Goodbye," we were on our own and stampeded out of the rattletrap building.

Two blocks away was another school, also German and parochial, only this was a branch of St. Mary's parish of the Catholic church. It was unavoidable that boys from the two schools met on the way home. Lutherans came face to face with Catholics and greetings were never friendly. In fact, both sides made a habit of tossing rocks. And of course everyone screamed. Unbelievable and unintelligible words. Occasionally my sister and her twin, not yet in school, appeared at the right moment, serving the cause by gathering and passing ammunition. It helped, but neither side ever won. Officer Stevens, who patrolled that beat, always made it a point to stroll by just as the fight got fiercest.

The war started in second grade and lasted all through it. The fall I entered Herr Professor Gerberding's room, the twins were to begin in first grade, and the day before school started a totally unexpected confrontation with St. Mary's occurred.

The three of us were alone when rowdies appeared in force near our home. They made remarks and Dorothy answered them. Another remark. Another answer. But the next word stung and the battle was on.

My mother heard the sounds, hurried out and waded into the melee, laying about her at friend and foe alike. Then she dragged her three into the house.

She lined us up on the living-room hearth.

"What were you fighting about?" she demanded.

"They called us a name," Dorothy said.

"What name?"

"I can't repeat it."

"Why not?"

"Because it's so terrible. It was a very dirty word."

"Very well. Don't repeat it. Try to forget it. But there is no reason at all for you to fight. You've got to learn to get along with people of all religions, all colors, all nationalities. You've got to learn to live in the world with them. Respect their beliefs and they will respect yours."

It might be good advice but it didn't take away the sound of the awful word. How could a decent person get along with people who talked to us the way the boys from St. Mary's had talked?

"There's absolutely no difference between you," my mother went on, trying to make us reasonable. "You come from the same kind of homes. You wear the same kind of clothes. You eat the same kind of food. Your fathers do the same kind of work. The only reason you don't all go to the same school is that they are Catholics and you are Protestants."

Dorothy, who had been crying, jumped quickly with horror in her eyes.

"We're *what?*" she demanded.

"It's just that you're Protestants and . . ."

"But that's what they call us! They call us dirty little Protestants! That's the *awful* word—Protestants!"

I remember the way my mother laughed, the way she tried not to and then laughed again. She looked at the three of us, still bearing the scars of honorable battle, clothes rumpled, faces soiled.

"I've never heard a truer description in my life, my dears," she said. "You're all that they say. You're dirty. You're little. You're Protestants."

We did not tell her that we had yelled "Dago worshiper!" and "Fish eater!" at our enemies. It did not occur to us to mention it. What offense could anyone possibly take at that?

"Suppose you invite some of the little Catholics from St. Mary's to come in and play," my mother suggested. "Bring the St. Paul Lutherans at the same time."

But a momentous event next morning made the suggestion impossible. School started. I was clean and brushed and had my high shoes on and was in my seat in Herr Professor Gerberding's room, behaving properly, when I heard a shrill scream from the first grade directly across the hall. Then another. And still another. They were cries of anguish, outrage and horror. They also were in my little sister's voice. I heard a scuffle, a stern German command to sit down, answered by another shriek of defiant rage.

Then Dorothy appeared in the corridor, running, her new books under her arm. Herr Professor Strieter was rushing after her, but she was faster and before he could really catch up, he had to turn. Brother Don had popped out of the door and was racing into the open air after Dorothy.

I could not be the only member of the family left, so I packed up my books and walked slowly home. I found my father in a fury. Herr Professor Strieter had hit Dorothy across the knuckles with a ruler, her first experience with corporal punishment.

Had any teacher ever hit *me?*

"Of course," I said. "They hit everybody, every day."

My mother was speechless. She merely sat shaking her head, and at long last demanded of me, "Why didn't you tell us?"

"Because everybody gets licked in school," I repeated.

My father said, "I'll go over and settle it." He neither pocketed a pistol nor tucked a blacksnake whip under his arm. He owned neither pistol nor whip. But he started out growling, and walked fast. In half an hour he was back. To my disappointment, his clothes were unruffled. There had been no fight; my suffering was unavenged.

"They are so stupid they didn't understand what I was objecting to," he reported. "Starting this afternoon, you are going to the Clay School."

My mother did not argue. Languages finally had lost. She said she would take us; she knew Miss Lloyd, the principal. So with the three of us in tow, she started the eight blocks to the Clay School before one o'clock.

It was elegant. It was clean. And there wasn't a paddle in sight. I fell in love with my teacher, with the twins' teacher too. They were beautiful Miss Slaughtery and even more beautiful Miss Irma Dochterman. I never missed *Der Kleine Katechismus.*

8

___

MISS JENNIE MURPHY
AND BUFFALO BILL

❀✦❀✦❀✦❀✦❀✦❀✦❀✦❀✦❀✦❀✦❀

B UFFALO BILL CODY's Mammoth Street Parade formed that
hot July morning near the old circus grounds on the Jail
Flats at the foot of Calhoun Street. The afternoon and evening
performances of the Genuine and Original Wild West Show
would be staged on the infield of Mr. Louis Centlivre's famous
Driving Park, a good mile farther north on Spy Run Creek. It
made a shorter parade to start from the Flats. But it was easier
on horses' hooves.

Posters plastered all over town had told for days of this
coming Stupendous Event. It would be a Powerful Drama
with Genuine Cheyenne and Deadwood Stagecoaches, the
Same Sioux Indians Who Slaughtered Brave General Custer at
Little Big Horn, Genuine Frontiersmen, Genuine Cowboys, a
Genuine Troop of the U.S. Third Cavalry. And let no one
confuse their Powerful Production, the posters warned, with
any lesser, second-class tent show. Nor confuse the Great
Buffalo Bill, Chief of the Scouts, Colonel Cody of the Western
Wars, with any second-rate Indian fighter. Here was the
West's Original Buffalo Killer.

Grandfather Goshorn had told the family stories of Buffalo
Bill the night before. Somewhere in his western wanderings
with transit and surveyor's chain, he had played poker with
the great Colonel Cody, more than once one gathered. Next

morning we left home soon after breakfast, Grandfather and I
first, the twins to follow with Father. The parade was to start
at eleven o'clock, but already Calhoun Street was filling. It was
hot and we walked slowly. Grandfather liked to, and I had to,
because I had on shoes. It was not a peculiarity of his, but
always of my parents, that if I went anywhere with any of
them I had to wear shoes.

Grandfather stopped frequently to shake hands with men he
hadn't seen for a few days, all of whom called him "Bill," and
who all said they would vote for him for surveyor again in the
fall. We reached Mr. Henry Auth's highly respectable saloon
with still thirty minutes before the parade, so we went in to
say "Good morning" to him, too, and to get out of the sun.
Grandfather leaned on the bar, slowly sipping a stein of cool—
not cold—beer, and I ate pretzels. "I know your father, my
boy," Mr. Auth said, pushing the huge bowl my way.

Crowds were thicker when we returned to the street, and
we were just about to find a place in the line in front of Mr.
Pellins' Drug Store when this apparition appeared. He wore
high-heeled boots and a pearl-gray Western hat much larger,
newer and more elegant than my grandfather's Western hat,
which was plain, rather rusty black. His gray, neatly trimmed
beard matched the hat, and his long gray hair hung in ringlets
from under the brim and spread across his shoulders.

Silver spurs sparkled on his shining, tall boots, silver ornaments on his buckskin shirt with fringes. A pair of silver-
mounted pistols dragged down the holsters that hung to his
silver filigreed belt. Also to his belt was fastened a loop of rope
that I knew must be his lasso.

Of course I recognized him. Any boy in town would have
spotted him at half a mile. Wasn't his picture on every bill-
board? He was, bar none, the most beautiful member of the
animal kingdom I ever had seen, and that included the pretty
actress friends of Uncle Gustave.

At the sight of my grandfather, this glass of frontier fashion
halted and stared. Then he held out his arms and rushed
toward us. "Bill!" he was yelling, "Bill!" My grandfather,
unable to think of anything more original to say, yelled "Bill!"

right back at him and they embraced, whacking each other on the shoulders and rumps.

Then my grandfather dragged me out of my fascinated immobility and said, "This is my grandson, Karl." And to me he said, "Shake hands with Colonel William Cody."

But the great man didn't shake hands with me. He patted me on the head, and I shamefacedly put my own hand back into my pocket. Then he smiled, and I forgave him. It was a nice smile, making fine wrinkles all over his face. His complexion was ruddy, about the color of a burning hay barn, and his nose seemed redder than the rest of him. Despite his plain delight at seeing my grandfather, and his elegant silver-spangled getup, he showed he was fretting about something.

It was about "that damn woman," I discovered as he began to talk, whose name was "Annie."

She had left her tent at seven o'clock that morning to make "some female purchases" at White's Fruit House, which wasn't really a fruit house but Fort Wayne's rather somber version of Macy's, Gimbel's, Kresge's, Western Auto and the A&P, on three crowded floors. She should have been back where the parade was forming long before this.

He went to the curb several times, glowering up and down the street. "Parade starts in two shakes," and next breath, "Can't wait for her another minute."

Then the woman appeared.

I did not like her. In fact, I disliked her intensely at once. She was carrying an armful of packages and wore the same kind of soft buckskin clothes that made Buffalo Bill magnificent, with dozens of strings of Indian beads around her neck. It was a thin neck and she looked terribly old. She wasn't pretty, like Uncle Gustave's actresses, not half as pretty as Buffalo Bill. Her eyes were dark, her hair was black and straight, and Colonel Cody introduced her to my grandfather as Mrs. Oakley.

"Hurry," the Colonel told her. "You're late."

She scowled, but started off quickly without answering, and the Great Man said, "She's a problem. All women are." Then he left us and we waited for the parade.

It seemed a long wait. Finally we heard the band, someone on the sidewalk started the applause and here it came—all the sound and sight and smell one had expected: creaking axles on the Deadwood Coach, sunlight sparkling on the instruments of the mounted band, soft clump-clump of hooves on the cedar-block paving, the horsey smell. Buffalo Bill's white charger was rearing and pivoting, but he paid no attention to its gyrations, just rode as if glued to the saddle, smiling and lifting the pearl-gray hat in gallant response to the applause. And bowed. Bowed to us, a lot of common people on the curb. It almost made up for his not shaking hands. I needn't tell anyone he had patted me on the head.

Mrs. Oakley, still looking out of sorts, was riding at Buffalo Bill's left, a pace or so behind him, on a smaller, mouse-colored pony that seemed to suit her perfectly. I still didn't like her. In fact, I liked her less. She turned and smiled, but it was *at* us, not *with* us.

That afternoon, in the Genuine Historical Pageant at the Driving Park, we saw the cavalry charge the Indians, saw Custer die again on the Little Big Horn, saw squaws by the dozen with papooses strapped to their backs, brave frontiersmen with long mustaches and long rifles, and whooping, shooting tribesmen chasing the stagecoach. And we saw Annie Oakley. We watched her shoot the daylights out of glass balls tossed into the air, shoot them standing, kneeling, lying on her back, cantering past on her mouse-gray pony.

I had to admit she was a good shot, almost but not quite as good as Grandfather Goshorn. There were no rattlesnakes for her to try to hit, and I was sure that she couldn't have shot all of them in the eye. Even if she did do surprising things with glass balls.

Cowboys bulldogged steers. Soldiers marched and counter-marched. Indians danced. Turkish Zouaves in red fezes and baggy pants trotted double time. "There weren't any Zouaves in the Wild West I knew," Grandfather said. Pawnees attacked the Deadwood Stagecoach and were driven off after much shooting. And all the time Buffalo Bill's horse danced to the music of the mounted band.

It was wonderful but it was the dramatic finale that pulled us out of our chairs. The Sioux had just finished off General Custer when the pioneer family came out of its log cabin in the middle of the arena—Grandfather said the logs were painted canvas—and was preparing supper over a fire when the dastardly Sioux attacked.

They charged around the field on horseback, yelping and firing their guns while the pioneers on their stomachs behind the horses fired back. Every now and again an Indian threw up his arms and tumbled dead. But the circle of savages closed in, a few feet at a time, and the helpless family was just about to be wiped out when hooves thundered at the far end of the infield.

The dashing Third Cavalry to the rescue. They saved the settlers but not until after an Indian had shot a blazing arrow to set the cabin's straw roof on fire. Cavalry and tribesmen rushed off, the frontier family withdrew and on a gallop from the sideline came Fort Wayne's own Engine Company Number Six, which had been waiting out back with steam engine and hose wagon. Captain Chris Royans' men put out the fire promptly, as fine a closing scene as anyone could wish. Buffalo Bill appeared again, rode once around the field, took off his hat, bowed, and told the crowd that he hoped his Genuine Wild West Show had been educational and entertaining. Then we went home.

My sister, who always before had played she was Florence Nightingale or the Princess of Zenda, took over the part of Annie Oakley next day and for months thereafter with a walking stick, broom or piece of lath demolished imaginary glass balls in our back yard. As a woman, Dorothy became an active pacifist, but at this point all she wanted was to be a good pistol shot. If she couldn't hit the imaginary balls, patient brother Don occasionally was the unintended victim.

The next morning I was in the kitchen good and early to tell Miss Jennie Murphy all about it. Miss Murphy did our washing and ironing and was not averse to taking a few minutes off now and again for conversation.

She listened to my story of the Wild West Show and then went to the stove and wet her finger and tested an iron.

"Shucks!" she said. "That all them Indians did? No scalping?"

"What's scalping?"

Miss Murphy sat down. She was a sickly looking woman with a cough and I knew, if my mother did not, that she always kept a bottle of "cough medicine" hidden in the pantry. When a coughing fit overtook her she would tip the bottle, swallow a large slug and then pat her spare middle appreciatively. This day she took two deep swallows.

"When I was a little girl out West," she said, "my whole family got scalped. My family was friends with General Custer, and when he heard about it he got so mad he went out and killed a thousand Indians."

My grandfather had never claimed friendship with General Custer nor had his entire family ever been scalped.

"Tell me," I demanded.

"When I was a girl we lived in a log cabin out on the prairie," Miss Murphy began. "We had a buffalo robe like the one your grandpaw has up in his room. We had lots of guns. Every day we had to fight off the Indians . . ."

I sat, fascinated, until Miss Murphy had finished the ironing, but the story of her privations and high adventure on the prairie was so long, so intricate, so fraught with terrors and suspense, that by six o'clock when she went home, she hadn't even got to the scalping. The next wash day she picked up the tale where she had left off. That night the Indians were just outside the cabin and the ammunition inside was running low.

It was the third week before her family got scalped and that was only the beginning of greater adventures.

"All got scalped except me," she said. "I was just a little child so I was spared and the Indians took me to live with them in their wigwams. I'll tell you about that next week."

The tale went on and on. Miss Murphy, never one to allow a sense of delicacy to rob a narrative of dramatic value, steeped me in settlers' gore. She rode with the warriors on forays against the whites; she attacked wagon trains; she finally escaped and fled across country, swimming rivers, leaping from cliff to cliff until she came to Wyoming. There, instead of taking a well-deserved rest, she cut her hair, put on pants, learned to smoke a pipe and joined the cavalry.

The story horrified and fascinated, and with the weeks, Miss Murphy grew in stature. Buffalo Bill and Annie Oakley and Florence Nightingale became mere homebodies, pale and dull and unimportant. Buffalo Bill had shaken hands with my Grandfather, Annie Oakley had shot glass balls, but that was impersonal. They weren't my close friends in my own kitchen. Here I needed only to reach out my hand and touch Miss Murphy, whose family had been scalped and who had lived in wigwams and worn pants and joined the cavalry.

That winter was the most lurid of my life. The next summer our family went north to Mackinac Island and I never saw Miss Murphy again. But I treasured her friendship and the memory of her stories; she was my closest personal contact with high adventure. Let other boys read their dime novels and get their thrills vicariously. I'd had Miss Murphy, right there by our own ironing board. Why I never mentioned this remarkable woman's adventures to my family, I do not know. Perhaps I selfishly was hugging the stories to my own bosom, keeping the thrills for myself alone. It was not until I was probably twelve years old that I heard the sequel to the tales she told.

One evening my mother looked up from the *Sentinel* and said, "Do you remember Jennie Murphy who used to wash for us? She died last night."

"Oh," I cried, "that's too bad!"

My mother had been talking to my father but she turned and looked at me curiously. "Do you remember Miss Murphy?"

"Of course," I said. "Her family got scalped."

"Got what?" my mother demanded.

"Scalped. By the Indians. While they lived on the prairie."

"Where did you get that ridiculous idea?" my mother asked.

"She told me all about it. When she was ironing."

"Well," my mother said, "the closest she ever got to the

prairie was Wallace and Hanna Streets out in Irishtown. She went to the Hanna School as far as seventh grade, then got a job in the Railroad Eating House. Her father was a street sweeper. I remember him well. Had red hair. Never looked to me as if he had been scalped."

Then to my father, she said, "I knew you couldn't believe what Jennie said when she was drinking."

"If she would tell the truth about her Uncle Charlie," he replied, "a certain young man's hair really would stand on end."

I wormed that story from Grandfather Goshorn merely by asking what had happened to Miss Murphy's Uncle Charlie.

"Lots of people would like to know," he said. "Skipped bail."

He explained what that meant.

"Long time ago," he went on, "year I came to town, Charlie ran a saloon on Railroad Avenue, back of the Pittsburgh depot. Big cellar under it. Hole in the ground now."

I knew the hole. Boys used to congregate and stare at it and tell or imagine what mighty blast had made it.

"Saloon was called Robbers' Roost," Grandfather continued. "Hangout for bad men. Pickpockets, burglars, footpads, horsethieves. Chiefly horsethieves. One night they robbed a man waiting for his train at the depot. Hit him on the head."

"Did he die?" I asked.

"No. But the railroad shopmen decided we'd had enough violence. So a crowd of five hundred or more went to Charlie's saloon. He escaped but they set fire to the building. Somebody called the firemen, but when they saw it was Robbers' Roost burning, they didn't even unreel the hose. Just enjoyed the show.

"Sheriff caught Charlie and his gang finally and locked them up. But a Chicago lawyer brought in nearly fifty thousand dollars cash and bailed them out. Charlie disappeared. Good riddance."

The town was well rid of him, I agreed. But I still felt sad about Miss Murphy. She had not robbed anyone and I had enjoyed her stories.

9

"NOBLE, UNPRONOUNCEABLE AND AWFUL"

✾⤳✪⤳✻⤳✪⤳✻⤳✪⤳✻⤳✪⤳✻⤳✪⤳✻⤳✪⤳✻⤳✪⤳✻⤳✪

THE INDIANS, with their facility for creating seducing sounds, had called the village where our three rivers met *Kekionga,* which they had corrupted from the even more musical *Kiskakon.* This supposedly was an Ottawa word, about which savants, who should know, have different opinions. They agree that the original word meant "to cut." But one group thinks it referred to the short tail of a bear, another that it described those fashionable Indians who shaved the sides of their heads and trimmed the rest of their locks like the manes of Roman horses.

Our local baseball team, which adopted the name *Kekionga,* probably didn't care whether they played like bears or wild horses. Both were ferocious.

At least *Kekionga* could not be translated into "Home of Skunks," as the name of poor Chicago could be; or "River of Wild Onion Smell," the Chippewa word for the village where I now live; or even plain "Stinks," as the native quarters of some of our outposts were called.

Whatever the beginnings, it could be left for the French pioneers, always particular about the pronunciation of their own peculiar words, to twist the Miami, Ottawa or other noble syllables they met into Gallic linguistics sharply divorced from their original meanings.

Many of the French words stayed a long time in our town, together with the baptismal titles of the earliest French *voyageurs* and settlers. But these, in turn, met their match in the Irish invasion. The Irish, with their free-and-easy disregard for propriety, practically wiped out the first families, linguistically at least. The proud Peltiers—who naturally had called themselves "Pelt-yea"—became "Pelkys." The Comparets—"Comparays" in their own opinion—turned into "Comparettes," which they remain on careless tongues today.

All the settlers imported strange nomenclatures that needed no mispronunciation to give them odd sounds. English, German, Irish, French, Norwegian, Italian, Polish, and don't forget the Scotch, all brought their own trademarks. They often were frightening enough.

The first marriage license granted in Springfield Township went to Washington Corpse, and a reckless young damsel soon after married Cy Hollopeter—not a difficult name to remember in a town that had Ungemachs, Melsheimers, Redelsheimers, Hochstaetters, Stoeppelwerths and Princess Kil-so-quah.

It took small boys and waggish adults to bestow undeserved monikers on some of their neighbors, and the less the neighbors liked them, the more firmly the names stuck. All the holy names of history notwithstanding, the real names could be less important than what certain folks were impolitely called on the street. For example, there was "Shakespeare." And Mr. Joseph Griffith, "Joe the Lion Tamer," with whom my mother unexplainably did not want me to shake hands. "Fowl" was what small boys, for some reason that seemed sensible to small boys, rudely called one Ernst Lange, corrupting *faul*, a German word for "lazy," to apply to the backward offspring of a reputable family. The honest burgher nicknamed "Schwäbenfritz" was a saloon keeper from Schwäbia, who found the syllables so musical that he added them to the sign outside his door.

Everyone in a kindly manner addressed little Charley Nestel, the midget, by his stage name of "Commodore Foote." He had performed with his sister before Queen Victoria, their

Royal Highnesses the Prince and Princess of Wales, King
Edward VII, Queen Alexandria, the Shah of Persia, ex-
Empress Eugénie of France, the kings of Zululand and the
Sandwich Islands, and he wore a real Guinea Gold Medal to
prove it. His assumed rank of "Commodore" no doubt resulted
from the Navy uniform, with epaulets, much gold braid and
all the brightly colored ribbons an imaginative tailor could
provide, that he wore before the gas footlights—he didn't need
any intimate past connection with water. His little sister
Eliza's nickname "Queenie" was more understandable. It was
after her dramatic title "Faërie Queen" and lasted her lifetime.

"The Woman in Black" was short-lived. Her name stirred up
plenty of talk for a period, in fact that town never in its life
had as frightening an experience, the entire West End going
into palpitations. This character, tall and chunky, clad in long
black skirts, black bodice and jacket, black bonnet and heavy
black veil, made a practice of hiding in hedges and behind
trees in the respectable area between Ewing Street and Swinney Park in mid-evening or later, and leaping out at passing
ladies venturing alone.

The apparition made no sound. She merely gripped the
scared-stiff victim and pinched her on the bottom, then fled
into darkness. Nothing more.

Police patrols were doubled. Gentlemen armed with canes,
baseball bats and golf clubs patrolled the area. They finally
waylaid "The Woman."

She tried to escape, but enraged males set upon her and in a
very ungentlemanly fashion tore her black clothing away,
disclosing no woman, just a supposedly conservative, local
professional man. He was having fun, he said. His shocked
neighbors released him and he tried to go about his affairs as
if nothing had happened, but something *had* happened, so he
finally left town and took the name of "The Woman in Black"
with him.

Uncle Gustave, skeptical as usual at the beginning, had a
good laugh when the villain was unmasked. Many of the
respectable females who had been "assaulted and humiliated"
were maiden ladies of his acquaintance, and he insisted that

they probably had never enjoyed anything in their lives as much as the pinches on their virginal bottoms.

My mother said, "Hush, Gustave."

The greatest name on the street, my generation thought, was "Shakespeare," which was not the wretched man's name at all, and never had been. Grandfather Goshorn always referred to him respectfully as Mr. James Mitchell, who many years earlier had been the fire-breathing editor of the Fort Wayne *Dispatch,* the persistant organ of the dying Greenback Party, with its devotion to "sound government money." Grandfather explained that poor Mr. Mitchell had fallen on unhappy times because he kept two bottles on his desk, one of ink, the other of aged Maryland whiskey, and in his editorials mixed them in equal parts. This was the reason why some days his writing was bright and full of color, another day fuzzy. It also helped account for his losing his newspaper, even before the Greenbackers deserted the ship themselves.

Another reason for Mr. Mitchell's permanent exit from the *Dispatch* concerned a society column one June, when in a gay moment of inspiration he jumbled the reports of two society weddings and the livestock market. He not only married off two innocent girls to the wrong men, clad each bride's mother in the other's gown, but then, having taken another slug of Maryland rye, added that the two nice-looking 165-pound heifers from Adams Township had brought fancy prices that day. This so delighted the whimsical-minded among his readers that one pair of the newlyweds moved to Xenia, Ohio, and the other to Toledo.

Just when Mr. Mitchell with his curly white whiskers became "Shakespeare" no one ever could remember. One story was that when he first came to town he quoted passages from the Bard on all occasions. Whether he earned the name or not, he resented it. Mr. H. H. Paramore of the rival *Evening Press* loved to chide him in print, fearlessly signing even his most libelous accusations against the Greenback editor, or anyone else, with a flourish; not with his own name, of course. But the whole town was aware that "Alas P. Yorick" was Editor Paramore.

None of the many phony signatures made much sense. Everyone knew who everyone else was. It was common knowledge that "Jack Dee" was John Dougal, a fixture on the staff of the *News;* that "Americus," who wrote fire-breathing letters to any and all editors, was just explosive Dr. Kent Wheelock; and the "Pope's Right-Hand Man," an affectionate title used by Catholics and Protestants alike on newspaper row, was not a man at all, any more than "The Woman in Black" was a woman. She was a devout, middle-aged maiden lady who turned in items by the thousands about Roman Catholic organizations and personalities that could not possibly all get printed.

Editor Mitchell never barged into the *Evening Press* sanctum with a cane or a horsewhip in hand, because it was no secret that Mr. Paramore kept a frontier model pistol in his roll-top desk. Had it been he, rather than Mr. Mitchell, who was called "Shakespeare," it would be understandable, but he was not, so one had to accept life as inexplicable and go on from there. Mr. Paramore retired to other scenes before I began to take notice, but every boy of my age knew Shakespeare well. Since he resented the name, all one had to do was start running, and then holler "Shake—speare!" and he did the rest. It was not safe to holler first and then start to run, for despite sixty-five misspent years and the soiled, ankle-length overcoat that he wore from Labor Day through Memorial Day, this sensitive character could give a yearling gazelle lessons in the mile run.

My first adventure with him began in front of Miss Rodenbeck's stylish, if somewhat steamy, hairdressing parlor, where I liked to pause to sniff the exquisite perfumes wafting through the door. The memory of them stayed with me always, so that whenever in my later youth I read the plaint of Lady Macbeth on "all the perfumes of Arabia," I was invariably reminded of the plump, pleasant, blond Miss Rodenbeck. I had paused one summer morning when Shakespeare came out of a bar up the block and turned in my direction, leaning heavily on his two canes.

Someone, somewhere, hollered, "Shake—speare!"

Not I. But I was the one Shakespeare saw. Naturally he pinned the guilt on me, and I took off across the cedar-block pavement. I had a fair start and I lived only two streets away, but he gained on me rapidly and suddenly for some reason I found myself running up the broad steps of the Cathedral of the Immaculate Conception.

I was not too familiar with its interior, but luck placed close at hand a curtained confessional not in use and from that cramped sanctuary I heard Shakespeare barge in. He was making a frightful racket, yelling after me, banging his canes against the prie-dieux between the pews, when an elderly priest, who apparently had seen me seek safety, touched the angry man on the shoulder, whispered sharply to him to remove his hat, sit down, keep quiet, and may God have mercy on his soul.

Of course Shakespeare became angrier than ever. He announced in a loud voice that he would allow no damned mackerel snapper to pray over him, but nevertheless he departed, still fuming. The priest, who had been a boy once, waited a moment to be sure the coast was clear, then quietly but firmly he removed me from the confessional and let me out a side door. I saw him occasionally on the street in the next few years, and whenever we passed, he winked at me but did not speak.

One time when Shakespeare did nearly catch me, I was exploring the alley behind the Randall Hotel, near the spot where Mr. Perry A. Randall, who was so rich he never needed to hunt for money, had found the brand new half-eagle gold piece in the mud. I wasn't rich, so whenever I had time I searched the alley diligently, but instead of five dollars all I ever picked up was a William McKinley campaign button badly scratched around the edges.

On this afternoon, I suddenly heard Shakespeare's voice afar off, creating the hullabaloo that starts dogs to barking. It was somewhere over toward the Nickel Plate railroad tracks at first, but it came on fast and he entered running, stage left, at the end of the alley. His whiskers, parted by the wind, streamed back past his ears. His overcoat floated out behind, his two knotty canes flailed. I forgot all about gold pieces and concentrated on survival. I would have to hide again in a hurry.

A number of places were available. Every boy knew them, snug harbors of refuge when needed. The streetcar barns in Chestnut Street combined safety from pursuit with imminent danger of electrocution, which gave them a special allure. Gilmartin's Lumber Yard on Barr Street was a labyrinth of hidden pockets, but the three employes, Pete, Mike and Isaac, took a dim view of all boys and liked to flush them out. There was also the belfry of old Third Presbyterian Church, which offered safety with a view. Nearest this time, though, was one of the finest sanctuaries in town. It was in Mr. Horstman's Livery Stable, fronting on Pearl Street, by way of the back door and under the old hearse by the rear wall.

In those days of pretentious funerals, a town's best example of artistic sculpture often could be found on a hearse. Mr. Horstman had several fancy ones in use for his better customers, but this one, originally a glorious work of art, had fallen on evil days. The sheet of beveled plate glass on the left side had cracked. The carved wreaths, urns and mourning doves along the top were chipped. The hard rubber tires were worn but the wheels turned without too much squeak and it still was used for second-class funerals in Irishtown or out on Hungry Hill. It helped make the dark back room in Mr. Horstman's stable plenty spooky, but with Shakespeare's canes threatening, any experienced youth would have charged the cannon's mouth. I ducked low, ran through the gloom, crawled under the hearse and waited.

Outside, Shakespeare lunged past in full cry. Mr. Horstman, attracted by the racket, left his game of cribbage up front and walked back slowly, hat on his head, to see what was happening. At the door he looked up and down the alley, took his derby off, smoothed his hair, then recognizing Shakespeare's voice, now far away, he chuckled, came back into the barn and closed the door. I ducked my head down to the floor.

No one in those uncomplicated days was said to be allergic to anything; in our town, and I am sure in most of its neighbors, the word had not been invented. Dry straw just happened to make some persons sneeze and I just happened to be one of them. Now as I huddled on the floor under the hearse, fearful of moving a muscle, I felt a sneeze coming on. I held my nose between thumb and forefinger. I held my breath, swallowed repeatedly, all to no avail. As I was about to choke to death and with Mr. Horstman's legs visible not five yards away, the sneeze erupted.

It even startled Mr. Horstman, who was not the kind of man to startle easily. He shouted, "Who the devil!" Bending low, he stared in at me, then stood up and began to pull at the hearse, dragging it out, creaking, by its tongue. That would give him a clear path at me; it also gave me an opportunity.

Before he could drop the tongue of the hearse, I had rolled over half a dozen times, cleared the clutter of carriage wheels and was headed for the broad front door. Seconds later I was far up Pearl Street in the direction opposite that taken by Shakespeare, and Mr. Horstman was standing in front of the Palace Stables, a buggy whip in his hand, looking after me.

That day was the last time I ever ran from Shakespeare. A few weeks later, a boy who should have known better had the poor judgement to holler first and then start to run. The old editor aimed swiftly and hurled the cane with the heavy silver knob. The boy was carried off to Hope Hospital to regain consciousness.

Shakespeare was arrested and dragged before Judge Ben Skelton in City Court. Judge Ben was a casual jurist who before mounting the bench had operated a little grocery on the South Side; so his mind was uncluttered with precedents and technicalities and he dispensed plain justice without frills. It was his proud boast that he had been among the first "to answer the call of Lincoln," and one reason the grocery had remained small was because, like many old soldiers, he had dedicated most of his time and intellect to the affairs of the Grand Army of the Republic.

Poor Shakespeare was most unfortunate in coming before Judge Ben, for the story whispered about town was that the ex-

editor's past included a hitch as a rebel soldier and that he had
fought on the wrong side at Shiloh and Pittsburg Landing.

Judge Ben had done his part at Shiloh, too, shoulder to
brave shoulder with Indiana's General Lew Wallace, not to
mention Judge Hench. Naturally Judge Ben could recognize
subversion when it appeared openly in court. So as Shakespeare stood before him in the damp basement courtroom in
the City Hall, the judge did his patriotic duty and Shakespeare
went to eat his meals at the County Jail for several months.
Where he disappeared to when he got out, no one ever knew
and I suppose never asked. At least he never again gave
drama, gaiety and high adventure to our streets.

Being a boy was less amusing after that. We still had "Joe
the Lion Tamer." And "Fowl." And scores of minor characters
who gladly would have chased anybody who cared to yell at
them. We still turned out en masse when "Commodore Foote"
made an appearance at historic anniversary celebrations. But
we had lost a certain fellow of infinite jest, a scarecrow in a
long coat who unwittingly made a great name contemporary.
A few young fellows I could have mentioned might even have
been surprised to learn that it belonged to anybody before
Editor Mitchell.

The name that really fascinated me was not contemporary,
and most people, after considerable clearing of throat, seemed
determined to forget it. Their attitude was, hush, don't soil
your tongue. If you don't mention such a scoundrel, maybe he
will go away, maybe he never lived here, never even lived
anywhere. Maybe it's just an old folk tale.

Simon Girty wasn't a saint; I learned that much easily. He
and his brothers had been spies and very clever ones. But was
that the reason so many respectable people didn't want to talk
about them? What was so wrong about spies? Captain William Wells had been a spy, and who in town failed to respect
his distinguished name? Many a local householder still gives
his home address along the meandering creek in the north part
of town as "Spy Run," and one long, respectable street is
named "Wells." He was an authentic American hero, so daring

that when the Miamis finally caught him, they roasted his heart and passed it around the dinner table so their young warriors could partake of it and of his courage.

People were willing and glad to talk about Spy Wells, but most of them refused point blank to answer any question about Spy Girty.

Even my grandfather just said, "Girty? Long before my time," and my mother, not so briefly, "A renegade American who worked for the British. An American Army lieutenant." The British were claiming the whole Northwest Territory, she added, and needed all the help anyone could give them.

The British had no right to the territory, even I knew, but wasn't there something else about this fellow Girty?

One teacher I asked just answered, "Girty? We're not studying that period now," and forgetting I was still there, she pointed at a girl across the room and said, "Next question?"

"His first name was Simon," my mother one day took time to tell me. "His brothers were George and James. Spies for the British, all three of them. Why are you so interested in him?"

I couldn't answer; I didn't know myself. Why I was interested was what I was trying to find out. He had left dirty footprints in our history, it was clear, and his name was far less respectable than Shakespeare's, but when I asked whether any descendants still lived in town, no one seemed to hear me. There was nothing with that spelling in the city directory and nothing in town was named after the family, not even a horse-drawn steam fire engine. It sounded like the kind of scandal that Uncle Gustave's *Evening News* should rush into print, even at this late date, and I finally wormed it out of Miss Jennie MacPhail, Miss Margaret's younger sister, who taught in the Jefferson Elementary School.

Each of the three brothers, Miss Jennie told me, weighing her words carefully, had "taken up with Shawnee women." When she continued, after a dramatic pause, she spoke almost in parables, from which I slowly understood that not only did each wicked brother sire numerous half-breed offspring, but that the climax of the story was even more ghastly.

"Every one of them," she whispered, "every one—died

intoxicated!" and she gave a particularly loud sniff. Clearly this was no way even for a Girty to stagger up the stair to meet his Maker.

"I can't imagine," Miss Jennie used to say, "why you keep talking about these despicable people when there are so many noble characters in literature or history. Particularly," she would add, "in the glorious history of Scotland."

The disclosure that there were many Girty progeny only stirred my curiosity. What had become of them? Did we pass these sons and daughters of Satan, unknowing, in the street? Could they belong to any of the several half-breed families still living out on the edge of town? Most of these were decent enough folk, who would not steal unless too greatly tempted, and one and all could be counted on to do an honest day's work; if properly supervised.

I gave up finally. I never met any of the family in the flesh. Either they had changed their names or moved to Wyoming.

I stopped asking questions about them finally; at the same time I became careful of the word. It didn't matter what you called most of your friends.

"Stinky" Bergman didn't mind his title, even if his mother did, and, no offense meant, we always had at least one "Sheeny" in our neighborhood. But no matter what the temptation, or how lively the argument at the moment, or how mean and underhanded the character, I never chased anybody down the street calling him a "Dirty Girty." Miss Jennie MacPhail had made that much impression on me.

10

HEAP O' LIVIN'

N O MATTER where we lived, our house always bulged with people. They were of every class, kind and color, every persuasion, conviction and economic level. They came from across town, across the state, across the Atlantic or Pacific, a few from "out West."

Invited or uninvited, they came to eat, sleep, read books, or just to sit in the living room discussing matters. Our big oak dining table had five extra boards to be called on in emergencies. They frequently were called.

Visitors included Democrats, Republicans, once an anarchist with whiskers, vegetarians who had to eat assorted nuts while the rest of us had steak, Moslems, Baptists, Theosophists who thought their grandmothers had been cats or dogs, single taxers, a wild-eyed crusading prohibitionist and for one long week two grim members of the River Brethren from the county in Pennsylvania where my mother had happened to be born.

One dusky gentleman, in the day or two he was with us, spoke only half a dozen words, politely, in what he imagined was English, and in spite of my sister's raised eyebrows, wore a fez at the dinner table, his mother never having taught him to remove his hat at meals.

The first of these strangers came to our big, "semi-detached" Victorian monstrosity on East Berry Street—three layers of tall, pure gingerbread with caramel frosting and colored glass panels above the parlor windows. Its round tower at one corner of the roof and the "oriental" bead portières in the golden oak archway between parlor and living room gave added touches of splendor, and on the front porch a row of spindles supporting a handrail were just far enough apart to pinion a curious three-year-old by the neck.

One of our houseguests there was a lady no one could forget. She had a mass of flaming red hair and smelled of perfume and complained about everything, including the innocent toy in which bells rang merrily when it was pulled across the floor. Most impressive was the fuss she made over a drink of a foul-smelling liquid called *koumiss* that a doctor in Philadelphia or Chicago or somewhere had prescribed. My father was unsympathetic, as he was toward most prescriptions. A druggist of long experience, he knew that the basis of many of them, and most "tonics," was what he called "rot-gut whiskey."

Years later I asked him about the lady and the *koumiss* and he said she was no lady and that *koumiss* was a fad, a sort of liquor distilled from fermented camels' milk. He had found some for her, he remembered; his druggist friend, George Loesch, had a little in stock. He reminded me that the visitor was no relative of his. She was a widow of a Greek who once worked for Grandfather Goshorn.

It was in this East Berry Street menage, shortly after the twins were born, that I first became aware of strangers in our midst. Of various ages, they moved in one day loaded with sacks, boxes and piles of clothing; and my mother explained that Fort Wayne's three rivers had gone over their banks and these were some of the victims. From that year on we could expect an invasion each February thaw when denizens of Wagner Street, Baltes Avenue and low-lying sections of the far western suburb aptly called "Nebraska" moved their choicer belongings upstairs and took to our hospitable beds. Not to mention board.

Of course, we were ready at all times for unexpected and often unexplained arrivals of relatives. That term spread over a great deal of territory, sometimes not even visible from the top of our family tree. My father was a kindly man, and although he was highly impatient with most pious frauds, he accepted as practically next of kin the divorced wife of a half-brother-of-the-husband of a second-cousin-once-removed. This made for far-out relationships—and house guests.

My mother, with her sympathetic heart, had the happy, extravagant faculty of learning not only of victims of floods, but of all man-made adversities, not to mention Acts of God. Her good fairy apprised her immediately of any unfortunate—often with five children—whose modest home had burned, been blown away by a tornado, shattered by lightning or blasted heavenward by leaking illuminating gas.

She was first to get the bad news when a family's mortgage had been foreclosed, its breadwinner shot in the back or sent to jail—or enticed into eloping with some hussy down the block. Almost automatically, she would rush home and turn down the beds in the spare room and set up a couple of cribs. Some of these temporary unfortunates became regulars, drifting to our door whenever trouble loomed, as naturally as my Uncle Fred drifted into the Hof Brau Haus Bar.

Several times my father's sister moved in on us, once bringing three large trunks and dozens of strings of beads. The strings were forever breaking, scattering the beads across the floor; and the younger generation must drop everything else, no matter how important, and crawl around and pick them up. We wouldn't want our poor old aunt to have to get down on her hands and knees, would we? We had been told to be exceptionally polite to this particular aunt. She had been a beautiful girl who had been widowed young and a victim of unkind fates ever since. Now, thin and frail, she deserved our sympathy, Father said. We gave it, but how generously depended some days on how many times a string broke and beads rolled on the floor.

There was an overweight, elderly lady, whose name I remember but shall not repeat, who crawled out of bed around three o'clock nearly every night and sang at the top of her healthy lungs. The day before she departed, my father told my mother, "I can take a great deal, Laura, without complaining. But if that woman doesn't get out of here, I shall." She never came back.

Another whom we called "Aunt Maggie" did come back frequently, and in spite of the fact that she was Mother's old friend and not Father's, it was Mother who most objected to her. "Aunt Maggie" was no aunt. She was a widow with peculiar black straw hats and frowsy gray hair who had taught in the Jefferson Grade School when Mother did, and therefore must be pitied. The time she stayed the night, she arrived after the younger generation was abed and made a terrible fuss at the door, awakening us and drawing us rapidly to the top of the stairs.

Under our fascinated gaze she screamed and fell down in the front hall, because, Mother explained next day, she had become suddenly very ill. Our father carried her up to bed, but he was not his usual courteous self. This time what he had to say, fiercely, he addressed directly to her, instead of just warning Mother. "Maggie, if you don't get quiet damn quick and stay quiet, I'll call the police!" She obeyed. We went back to bed, missing regretfully the high adventure of an arriving patrol wagon.

All the youth in the neighborhood enjoyed Aunt Maggie, the only lady who joined enthusiastically in louder, more strenuous back-yard games. She even hitched her long, gray skirts and climbed on the fence to hoot derisively at Pete, Mike and Isaac in Mr. Gilmartin's lumber yard that backed up on our lot. They never hooted back, merely put down the planks they were stacking and looked astonished. Isaac often tipped his cap politely. But if she fell off the fence on their side, instead of rushing to grab her the way they tried to grab us, all three fled in the opposite direction.

Aunt Maggie took falls in good humor, never accusing boys of pushing her, as many girls did. To our astonishment, sometimes in the midst of a game, just standing on smooth earth, she fell flat on her face. But she never got hurt, merely rolled over, staggered to her feet and went on with the game.

We felt that our mother did not always treat her well. She never threatened as Father did to call the police, but often, when she heard Aunt Maggie coming, she would lock herself in the bathroom, usually with a good book, and not come out until our guest was long gone, merrily trilling as she weaved her uncertain way up the street.

I had been born on West Wayne Street in a two-story red-brick house that still stands, although it is now more than a hundred years old. It looked trim and solid when last I saw it, a tasty architectural melange of styles, leaning on the shoulder of good Queen Anne, and on the whole rather handsome. If anything exciting happened in it, besides my arrival, I was too young to enjoy it. In East Berry Street, I do remember excitement. The old frame Clay School, two blocks away, burned one cold February night in 1894, and my father wrapped me in a comforter and held me at an attic window. I saw flames and a dark figure on a ladder, and was happily conditioned to be a life-long firebuff.

East Berry was eminently respectable, its maple and buck-eye trees shading fine Victorian houses and an occasional big "homestead," plus a few new McKinley-Modern residences like the one we rented. A few blocks west of us, the Court House, Post Office and City Hall gave the street prestige, and a block north was triangular Old Fort Park where on Decoration Days we honored Anthony Wayne.

People flocked to the East Berry Street mansion in our more prosperous times, and when times were bad, a few came to the shabby little house in Douglas Avenue that smelled of escaping gas. It was the poorest in a short block of plain, modest houses typical of the 1890s. All of muddy Douglas Avenue did not stretch a quarter mile. Its name was a relic of Civil War days, when the gusty little Democratic Senator who debated Abraham Lincoln paraded through town, stirring hot support of his "half free, half slave" policy.

Indiana proudly claimed Lincoln's boyhood, but at least

until the Civil War was declared, she was "ag'in the government" as to slavery. Our town not only named a street for
Senator Douglas; along with the rest of the county it voted for
him over Mr. Lincoln, by a good margin; I never heard anyone
in school allude to this embarrassing fact. Teachers merely
asked us to memorize the Emancipation Proclamation and
learn the dates of Gettysburg and Appomattox.

Nor did any teacher confess what I discovered later, that
just forty years before I was born, our freedom-loving citizens
voted, six to one, to bar the black man from our county, at the
very moment city fathers petitioned the legislature to help
import good labor from Europe. What I did not learn of true
democracy in class, I did learn at home; so when in the new
Clay School, Sam Jones, son of a colored porter, was my
favorite classmate and came to play billiards on our lumpy
table, my mother usually invited him to supper.

Our parents were not happy in Douglas Avenue. A cloud of
uneasiness, dark enough for a child to sense, hung over the
house. We had been living on East Berry when in a local
election, despite the fact that the county was Democratic—
Grover Cleveland had just taken it two-to-one—my ill-advised
father was persuaded to mortgage his drug store, the biggest
and most modern in town, to raise money to run as a Republican for county treasurer. He lost by 281 votes, not only the
election but the store, and for a time doggedly mixed his own
creams and lotions in a shed behind our house, peddling them
afoot to local druggists. It was to be his only venture into
politics.

In spite of our straitened finances, or because of them, the
people on Douglas Avenue were friendly. Directly opposite us
lived Mr. O'Rourke, a "rising young lawyer" and his son Allen
who was one year older than I. Occasionally Allen would
glance at me, and when he did my day was made. Next door
to the west, in a house twice the size of ours but painted the
same drab gray, dwelt two bachelor printer brothers, their
spinster sister, and the sister's friend, a pretty dark-eyed
woman who clerked in Mr. DeWald's Dry Goods Store.

All were "gainfully employed" and were neighborly folk

who on occasion sent pies and puddings to our house, where such frivolity was most appreciated. Beyond them in a solid brick house on the corner, also painted gray, lived an elderly gentleman with curly whiskers and crinkly eyes who had been a judge and was very important, but not so important that he didn't like children. At times he invited us to sit on his porch and listen to his music box play "Dear Evalina" and "Juanita."

Across the alley to the east, in a big red-brick house with wrought-iron railings and many lightning rods, lived Mr. Helmke, a quiet, German-born gentleman in a round black hat who owned the three-story "Helmke Block" on the corner beyond. I thought him a very rich man, collecting a fortune in rents. In his building were Mr. Christian's drug store, where a yard of licorice cost one cent, next to it Mrs. Warner's millinery with ostrich plumes in the window, and just beyond it the Notions Shop. Two old ladies, who dressed alike in what my mother called black bombazine, operated this emporium and to it regularly Mother sent me with a handful of small change for needles, Coates' thread or buttons as she or Mrs. Hagerhorst needed them.

Mrs. Hagerhorst, the seamstress, was a fixture for years, creating everything from pajamas to kneecaps with hand needle or sewing machine in our upper hall. Kneecaps were heavy cloth shields worn over the knees where stockings and short pants met. Held in place by elastic strips fastened with shoe buttons, they served their purpose well. With Mr. Theodore Thieme's Pony-Stockings-for-Children selling at twenty cents a pair, protection was a serious matter. Whether one fell on brick sidewalks or merely crawled on them, stockings needed constant replacement if kneecaps were not worn.

Mrs. Hagerhorst also hemmed sheets and pillowcases, hacked old bath towels into washclothes, cut Father's worn trousers into short pants, and Mother's skirts into perky little dresses for sister Dorothy. This ancient, loyal woman, who could have taught Weber and Fields fine points of German-American accent, walked from her home on Wall Street—and the name of the street should not give any false ideas about her financial status. According to rumors, she sprang from a family much superior to Hans Hagerhorst, but there had been another of those "youthful tragedies," and she had married him.

Hans caned chairs. Fat, ruddy and contented, he sat all day with a stein of beer on his workbench and sang German songs while he wove thin strips of cane in and out. We youngsters in turn sat beside his wife as she sewed, listening to her horrendous accent, and when she was gone for the night, we amused ourselves by discussing the characters in her conversations, using her *schnitzelbank* diphthongs and *Münchener lager* vocabulary.

What caused such delight in our horrid young souls? We were taught to honor and respect our elders, whether they were named Schlaurendorf or Schnickelgruber. But "Hagerhorst" had a merry lilt, even if it lacked some of the fine flavor attached to "Horstman." This gentleman, whom we thought appropriately named, broke wild chargers with bridle and curb bit and a long training rope, in the alley behind the stable where I had hid from Shakespeare. His most unruly beast, moreover, was "fit for a lady to drive in three weeks."

Mrs. Hagerhorst did not weigh more than ninety pounds, even in her long string of jet beads and heavy steel-rimmed spectacles. Her husband, Hans, on the other hand, liked pork gravy and *apfelstrudel* and had a bay window of heroic proportions, a German *dichbauch*, which witty patrons in Uncle Martin's drug store called a "Milwaukee goiter."

"Why Milwaukee?" Uncle Gustave repeated my question. "Because beer is made there, too. Almost as good as Fort Wayne's."

The ancient foot-treadle sewing machine that Mrs. Hagerhorst used stood by a window in an upstairs hall in one of our more comfortable houses. It was not the first machine that Mr. Isaac M. Singer ever patented, but the second or third, perhaps, and some museum must now be displaying it. Its needle was a deadly dart if a talkative woman brought her foot down too heavily on the treadle while fussing with the cloth or thread. And since Mrs. Hagerhorst must talk, she finally one day stitched the needle to the end of her finger and young Dr. Hamilton, who lived in the next block, had to be called. We stood by, entranced, listening to a flow of German-American moans and curses about the *schrechlich gestinken* machine, while Dr. Hamilton, a dignified young medic, released the pressure foot and extracted the needle.

"If you had made her get quiet, you could have done it yourself," he told Mother with a show of impatience.

Mother, who met most emergencies calmly, had no retort. How could one silence Mrs. Hagerhorst?

From Douglas Avenue, we moved two blocks to a much larger brick house with a slightly less exclusive address on Montgomery Street, with a screened upstairs front porch. Here, on hot summer nights the family sat semi-shielded from the public, forced to hear, whether interested or not, all the small, intimate talk of people passing on the sidewalk below. Late travelers bound for the Pennsylvania station five hundred feet away, carrying their heavy bags, used to run past panting, to my father's annoyance. He hated tardiness. "If they would only start five minutes earlier, they wouldn't have to run," was the advice he applied indiscriminately to everyone all his life.

There were few places to play in the Montgomery Street house or in the fenced back yard, at the foot of which was an abandoned wood shed with an objectionable smell, probably from the rats in the alley.

Our alley was exceptional, we thought, not because of the rats—every alley had rats—but because on the other side of ours, in a red-brick barn, an old gentleman kept and cherished a "genuine," weatherbeaten stagecoach that in the days of the old Fort had carried the mail west. On a promise to be careful, he allowed us to pull it out of its stable, fill it with little girls, six inside and four on top, convert ourselves into hostile tribesmen and attack from all directions.

The front parlor, sitting room and dining room of the house all were small, though all boasted platoons of shiny bay windows; not beautiful, mother admitted, but valuable because they let in sunlight. Inside the windows in the sitting room most of the space was taken up by my Grandfather Goshorn's immense leather chair, with the buffalo rug in front of it to keep drafts off his gouty feet. From the middle of each ceiling hung a gas chandelier and on the walls the jets, with etched globes, were folded back when the flame was not burning.

It was in this house I met oriental rugs. Uncle Gustave brought the first, and then my mother, saving carefully, collected enough cash to send an order off to his favorite store in New York.

In contrast to the small rooms, the entrance hall was oversized. Two bedrooms could have fitted into it with space to spare for an extra bath. A wide, angling stairway and fashionably carved banister and balusters covered parts of two walls. A small fireplace, with gas log and glazed tile face, supported a mantel of quarter-sawed oak, topped by oak pillars surrounding a half-circular mirror, into which a boy could look only by climbing on a chair.

In front of the mirror stood the Venus de Milo, perhaps two feet tall. My Uncle Martin in the parlor above his drug store had a slightly smaller Venus, but she wore a natty, gilt clock in the middle of her tummy, with a thumbscrew for winding sticking out of her back. I thought this was a peculiar place for a clock but I never heard comment on it until one day, as we crossed the street following a brief visit to the flat, I heard my father ask my mother whether she had noticed Uncle Martin's Venus. I remember her one-word reply. "Fetching," she said, and I wondered for years just what she meant. After two or three years we moved thankfully into a pleasant house on Barr Street that my mother designed to fit the needs of our particular family and visiting friends.

Miss Margaret Hamilton, daughter of pioneer Allen Hamilton, who had reached Indiana in the 1820s by way of Kentucky and the Ohio River—aunt also of bicycle-riding Miss Edith—owned and lived in the old Hamilton Homestead, occupying all of what was rapidly becoming a downtown block. My mother and she long had been friends. They called formally on one another, lent books, exchanged clippings from *The Boston Transcript* and *The New York Herald,* and over tea—no one did social visiting on a telephone!—they chatted about new books, old prints and the tragic state of the drama in America.

It was generous Miss Hamilton who had given the growing town its first public "reading room." To spend tax money for books was wasteful, early city fathers had thought. So with her family's help, she had rented a small building, supplied a thousand books, and appointed my mother librarian, a post she held until she married. When the city council finally found the money, it became a "public library." But it had not been at first. Miss Hamilton was a dedicated feminist. Only ladies could enjoy her reading room or borrow books.

Miss Hamilton owned our Montgomery Street property, which she rented at a reasonable fifteen dollars a month. Now she suggested that Mother plan another house for the corner of the Homestead block, close by the Art School. Rent would depend on size. For the new big living room, dining room, kitchen, butler's pantry, six bedrooms and bath, the rate, the two women agreed, would be upped from fifteen dollars to twenty-five dollars a month.

It was a comfortable dwelling, with a wood-burning fireplace in the living room, an innovation in the day of the gas log and Indiana natural gas, and we children had our own bedrooms. But the favorite spot was the attic at the top of narrow stairs.

This was undivided, unplastered, cold in winter, hot in summer, dusty in all seasons. In one corner stood the rainwater tank, a huge, square, wooden affair that stored the water from the eaves and sent it under gravity pressure to bathroom and kitchen sink. In another corner were boxes of belongings, trunks, outworn furniture. The rest of it was Sherwood Forest, the deer park at Zenda, Manila Bay, and an island cave on the broad Mississippi. It was a land of enchantment.

Each morning in the hysterical era of the Spanish-American War, we raced up to an attic window to hang the flag to a pole sticking out from its sill. It was not until World War I that my father solved the daily problem—he nailed the flag to the pole, "to stay until the boys come home."

The attic might be magnificent, but the grounds on which

the Homestead and our new house stood were paradise. Around four sides was a high, iron picket fence that furnished neighborhood children a dangerous, therefore popular, place to climb and jump. The east half of the lot had been "allowed to run wild," and except for the old hay barn in one corner and a coach-house-turned-art-school in the other, consisted of a small thicket of hawthorne, lilac and cedars and a broad expanse of open field.

The barn, abutting the sidewalk at the far end, had a slate roof. So on days when there was nothing better to do, Whitey Robbins and I, Sam Jones and Sam Taylor, son of a Pennsylvania shop foreman with one leg, delightedly threw pebbles down on passersby. They never threw anything back, as we hoped; they merely glanced up, astonished that anyone could act so disgracefully in such respectable-looking premises.

The town was growing fast. There were new knitting mills, a new shirtwaist factory, a new company that made "self-measuring fuel pumps" for the new automobile trade, and to fill the new jobs new people came to town, bringing new children with them. To make room for a new high school, the board of education suddenly condemned the east half of the Hamilton block.

We could not give up our new house. So we moved it, intact, attic and all, two and a half blocks to the corner of Clinton and Holman Streets, across from the Pennsylvania shops.

This was an exciting episode, for while the movers inched it along by day on big rollers, we continued to sleep in the attic at night, eating our meals in Mrs. Brown's boarding house across the street and using her bathroom. Mr. Gilmartin's lumber yard covered a quarter of the block to which the house was moved. Two other dwellings were there ahead of us, along with several vacant lots, one still marked by the crumbled foundation of an old synagogue. The new yard began as a thicket of tall weeds, but by the time it was smooth and sodded, the place looked livable.

The adjoining piece of real estate, perhaps two hundred by three hundred feet, touching the lumber yard, was perfect for baseball, for Mr. Gilmartin, who distrusted boys, built a ten-foot fence that made a fine backstop. It was by far the loudest and busiest lot in the neighborhood. Brown Trucking Company drivers constantly had to calm their teams, skittish over our shouts, or rein them in fast, to keep from trampling outfielders after long fly balls.

It wasn't a fine yard like the old Hamilton grounds, but we liked it, and went into black despair when our mother, Miss Hamilton and some of their friends not only made it the city's first public playground, but put in a public wading pool, from which longer-legged boys must forever rescue toddlers out of twelve inches of water.

The public playground was quieter, but it encouraged juvenile delinquency because, unable to play baseball, we had to find other, and sometimes immoral entertainment. This included excursions into the forbidden lumber yard and the hilarious adventure of escaping from Pete, Mike and Isaac. Also it led to a new game, played always in the dusk on sidewalks far enough from home to shield us from suspicion. We stretched across the walk at the height of a man's shoe a length of good stout dark cord, borrowed from Mr. Jacobs of Adams Express Company, anchored it with a pair of empty tomato tins tied at each end, then lay out of sight in the bushes and waited.

Citizens, hurrying home from work or running for trains at the nearby depot, became entangled in the twine. The tins made a wonderful racket and, hidden, we learned many new words as the victims tried to extricate themselves or pick up luggage. Fortunately for both sides there were never any broken bones.

Besides Miss Amelia, the magnificent maid of all work, and I mean all, our family by this time consisted of two parents, the twins, the new brother, and myself. Then in addition to the Grandfathers and Uncle Gustave, there was the dog, or two dogs and a cat, and sometimes for a few brief enchanting days, four or five dogs. The permanent ones were fox terriers, which some people who got dogs mixed up with high fashion did not think as stylish as Boston terriers. They were Kinny, short for Skinny, a name our mother had not liked, and Betty, a maiden-lady dog who in her infancy had been protected against progeny and therefore was fat and sedate. For a time also, there was Napoleon, tiny and imperious, whom we naturally called Nap.

The extra dogs were strays. They followed us home when we patted them on the street, and we fed them in the cellar until our distracted father led them, one at a time, to the Humane Society. As soon as possible, we found more.

A low point in his life must have been the night he arrived home tired from a week of selling drugs and found eleven extra dogs in the basement, including one brownish mongrel, unusually fat in the middle, that the twins had decided to name Tommy. Mr. Ed Woodworth, a lawyer friend who had chanced by, said Tommy's name really should be Tomasetta, and sure enough, before Dad could get to the Humane Society next day with Tommy, there were eight new pups in the basement. We rarely heard our father swear. Occasionally he might yell, "Oh, my God!" in a loud voice and then look around quickly as if to explain that he was praying, not swearing; but he outdid himself the morning we led him down to see the eight healthy little newcomers in the box behind the furnace.

Of the six uncles on my father's side, two were bankers and two ministers of the gospel, the gospel being honest Lutheran. The two bankers were fun-loving Uncle Gustave, who never tried to teach us any thrift, and Uncle Ed, who would have been willing, had we consented to listen, to teach us important facts about stocks, coupons and bankruptcies.

This does not mean that Uncle Ed was concerned only with money, for on memorable Sunday afternoons he always arrived with a two-pound box of Mr. Gus Aurentz' candy under an arm and after supper joined us at the piano and taught us all the new song hits from Herald Square. I remember the night he introduced us to the rollicking, "Meet Me in St. Louis, Louie, Meet Me at the Fair." That was my second contact with the St. Louis Exposition. The first had been through Architect Sim Mahurin, who designed the Indiana building and invited us to see it. School kept me at home. I had to make do with a glass replica of the building my mother brought.

The two minister uncles could visit us frequently because they carried, just as Grandfather Adam had, annual passes for free coach fare anywhere on all railroads, reason enough for a boy to consider studying for the church. Actually, my father explained, railroad magnates Jim Hill, Jay Gould and Commodore Vanderbilt distributed the free passes not merely out of devotion to Christian ethics. They also were insurance that the clergy of all denominations would sensibly continue to distinguish right from wrong, patriotism from revolution, in the nasty, unreasonable strikes of trainmen, switchmen and shopmen that were beginning to disrupt railroad schedules, not to mention profits, all over the country.

Of the two preacher uncles, we respected Adam and admired him as the best fisherman and the best storyteller in the family. But Fred we children disliked. This was probably because he insisted on speaking in German—he preached in that language all his life, even through World War I. None of us could understand him. Also he had a very loud voice, credited as the farthest-carrying in Niles Center, Illinois. We may have inherited this dislike. My mother, who had neither brothers nor sisters, did not insist that my father's six brothers be good all the time; but when they were not, she wanted them to sin with gaiety and in a light, debonair manner. Uncle Fred's manner was never debonair, and besides, low German accents distracted her.

Uncle Fred did not come often nor stay long when he did, using our guest room merely as a dormitory, dividing his days pleasantly among the Hof Brau House, the Germania, Hoffman's Cider House, the Berry Buffet, and the dreary pastoral offices of German Lutheran ministerial friends. He paid little attention to the younger generation, until one spring he turned up unexpectedly with a basket of baby rabbits. To our joy, when he departed noisily next day, he left them on the side porch. To our dismay, next morning the rabbits departed, too. They would be much happier, my father explained, out at

Miss Lizzie Roebuck's farm, separated from our new grey-hound Kip, which was short for Rudyard Kipling.

Naturally there could be no choice between Kip and rabbits. We could no more turn him out than step over an abandoned baby. He had come to town with Mr. Barnum's circus and had been left with the local veterinarian suffering from pneumonia. It was the week that Rudyard Kipling had developed pneumonia somewhere in New England, and the morning and evening papers printed bulletins on his condition.

We always were particularly glad to see our Uncle Carl, who was not a preacher and was handsome like his brother Gustave, and as reckless as he in the way he passed out largess. On special occasions, because he came seldom, this might even reach the magnificence of a silver dollar; and once, as his namesake, I received on my birthday a five-dollar gold piece dated 1891. He told stories of New York and London and Tokyo, where he had connections with Big Business; and he never delayed matters at table, when we were perishing with hunger, by prayers of endless gratitude for what Providence had set before us. In fact, on the Lutheran side of the family, Uncle Carl was a religious outcast or worse. Part way through Lutheran divinity school, he had abandoned his father's church to become a godless Catholic.

Uncle Carl brought prints to mother from Japan. They filled any empty space on the walls of the living room and hall in the Clinton Street house. Space was at a premium. Books had first chance, on open shelves hammered together by my father from eight-inch boards from the nearby lumber yard. He never was able to keep ahead, for my mother not only was a silent partner in the local book shop and able to buy at cost, but she prowled junk shops, second-hand stores and even the rival bookstore, and brought home armloads.

Books overflowed tables and chairs and once, for a long time, there was a high stack in the corner of the living room. Even Amelia, the maid, after a little training, found nothing wrong in leaving it there.

THE EAST BERRY STREET GANG AND A SLIGHT CASE OF ARSON

I DON'T say that juvenile delinquency did not exist in Fort Wayne in that simple era when the infant twentieth century was beginning to take notice, but it certainly made no headlines. Our good police chief, Mr. Homer Gorsline, and our sheriff, Mr. Al Melching, a cheerful man who became a successful undertaker after being defeated for re-election, would not have recognized a "juvenile" or a "delinquent" had they come out of our back alley and thrown stones at them.

Both men knew a great deal about bad boys, however, for the woods and fields were full of them. Not wicked, just bad. A few of us, I still believe, were neither; not bad or wicked, simply ingenious. Certain morose citizens might not have appreciated the signs of youth, and sometimes we even got into the newspapers, not by name, but by uncomplimentary, albeit accurate, descriptions.

After one particularly amusing adventure, the awful details of which I am happy to forget, the *Journal Gazette* referred to "the work of the East Berry Street Gang." My friends and I clipped out the item. It was a proud but rather frightening moment for all of us. What if a parent or two did a little startled guessing? Not many small boys lived on East Berry Street. Actually we were not a gang. We were just the ener-

getic sons of a druggist, a traveling salesman, a doctor of
divinity, a bicycle repairman, a popular plumber and a few
other respectable citizens.

We never fell into the clutches of the law. On the whole the
law must have been rather understanding of us, and we of it,
for it was rumored among us that even policemen had been
boys once. Since our town was a county seat, we had two sets
of official law enforcers, not including the much-too-inquisitive
Truant Officer, who unfairly reported all transgressions to the
schoolboard.

The town police carried a bit more weight with us because
they wore uniforms and the sheriffs never did, except for their
big black hats, fedoras, not Western style. The town police
also had the distinction of driving a paddy wagon. This was
not known as a "Black Maria," as in more ordinary places, but
as the "Lily," because the first person hauled off to jail had
been a kicking and screaming lady named Lily.

Horses and wagons were housed cozily on the first floor at
the rear of the City Hall, handy to the lockup. A few fussy
persons complained that the barn down below made the
second-floor Council Chamber, a somber, quarter-sawed oak
room with Axminster carpet in the aisles, smell to high heaven,
and if that smell wasn't enough, the lockup competed in
redolence. The sheriff, in a business-like office just inside the
Main Street door of the Court House my Grandfather Goshorn
built, had no such trouble with smells. He had no horses and
his jail was in a separate building half a mile away.

The Hamilton pioneer, Allen, had been the county's first
sheriff. His respected family, whose name figured so largely
down the years in the community, multiplied its first holdings
many times over, but not from the first sheriff's wages. Records
show that he collected fifty dollars a year, which even then
would not have bought a team of Percherons, for duties
covering everything from arrests for trespass, gambling and
horse-stealing, to stopping a fight and making everyone, including popular office-holders, obey the liquor laws.

The fact that the first Hamilton had been a sheriff seemed
terribly important to me. In addition to Mr. Melching, the

sheriffs in my own time—remembered partly because their red-brick fortress of a jail stood across from the city ball park—were George Stout, Jesse Grice and Aaron Reichelderfer, who came along about the time I reached my teens.

Sheriff Stout did not pretend to be interested in anyone under voting age; we repaid him handsomely with complete indifference to him. Sheriff Grice, on the other hand, was a fine gentleman with a big gray mustache like the wing of an overfat pigeon and he wore a treacherous, undersized wig that tried to take off in the gentlest zephyr, so that he had to clamp it firmly in place with his left hand whenever he stooped down for me to shake his right. Sheriff Reichelderfer was my favorite.

The word "Reichelderfer" might roll liltingly off some peoples' tongues, but it caused Colonel Andy Moynihan, owner-editor of the *Journal Gazette*, deep distress when he tried to fit it into a headline. "What the county really needs," I once heard him tell his city editor, Tom Bresnahan, "is a sheriff named Kelly."

Sheriff Aaron was a lanky man who wore his badge seriously. He always walked with his head thrust forward like a bloodhound's, even when he was just going over to the Hof Brau House for lunch. He had the complexion of a four-alarm fire bursting through the roof, and his dark mustache was inclined to droop at the ends when the fall rainy season was on. He was said to use his high leather boots with dexterity on any enemy of the people who tried to crown him with a brass cuspidor, and if not his boots, then his broad-brimmed black hat. Once when he was summoned to settle a philosophical discussion that was drawing blood in the Palms Sample Room back of the Nickel Plate depot, he slipped in quietly through the Family Entrance in the rear, snatched off the hat and with it knocked down two large, angry men with one broad swipe. It was an expensive hat, too, and very becoming.

I remember a story of how Sheriff Reichelderfer once arrested a country preacher on a charge best forgotten, and the preacher no sooner landed in jail than he began to pray loudly for the soul of Aaron Reichelderfer. This may have been reasonable enough; the sheriff hadn't led a dull life. But

what the poor preacher didn't know, and Aaron did, was that
no matter what his own convictions were, his ancestors had
been strict church-going people. They not only had started the
first Sunday School in their swampy township but walked
barefoot to it every Sabbath and put on their shoes when they
got there, carefully taking them off again after three or four
hours when they started home in the mud. So when this
preacher under arrest began to pray for the sheriff, Aaron
began to pray even louder for the preacher, to the delight of
all the drunks in the tank. Emergencies were Aaron Reichelderfer's meat.

"The East Berry Street Gang" never had a head-on en-
counter with Sheriff Reichelderfer or Sheriff Melching or Chief
Gorsline, even if poor "Shakes–peare" did. This was because
"Shakes–peare" chased us, and not the other way round. Nor
did *we* chase Dr. Daisy Young. We hurled the snowballs, with
or without stones in them, and he pursued us hither and yon.

Dr. Young was the object of our special solicitation due
chiefly to his elegance. He had appeared in town one afternoon unannounced, rented an office that formerly had been a
pants-pressing shop and introduced himself by publishing
advertisements in the *Evening Sentinel*, the most pious of our
daily papers—E.A.K. Hackett, widely known as "Brother
Hackett," ran a daily Bible verse across the top of his front
page, but never refused an advertisement.

Dr. Young's "professional announcements," always three
columns by eight inches, were illustrated with a rather flattering pen-and-ink portrait of the man himself, smiling and
looking taller than his actual five feet, three inches. He was a
famous physician-surgeon, lately of Chicago, he asserted in
eighteen-point type, and he had come to Fort Wayne because
it was exactly the kind of wonderful town he had always
wanted to call his own. And now that he had set up shop, he
was ready to guarantee to cure all such "female complaints
and weaknesses" as plagued the good ladies of the community.

In fact, he stated, he was a graduate of a famous medical
school in Oklahoma Territory, and had been tutored by several distinguished Indian medicine men as well. Our own Dr.

Deming promptly insisted that he had examined a list of all the medical schools in America and found no trace of Dr. Young's alma mater. But everyone knew that Dr. Deming would believe the worst of any physician or surgeon who bought newspaper space to inform the public of himself or his skill.

Our snowy assaults on Dr. Young had nothing to do with the kind of medicine he practiced, or where he went to school, or with any type of complaints or weaknesses, female or otherwise. He just offered a magnificent, irresistible target. For Dr. Young wore gray striped pants, a clawhammer coat, high-buttoned black patent-leather shoes, faun-colored spats and daubed himself with perfume. To make him still more enticing, he sported a white carnation in his button hole, even in winter. Mr. Ernie Rurode, our merchant prince, wore his carnation to Trinity Lutheran services on Sunday, but Dr. Young wore his every day, rain or shine.

To make matters still more tempting, there was the doctor's crowning glory, a pearl-gray stovepipe hat tipped slightly back and to the right. He was no coward, for he wore it even in good snowball weather. But the hat settled it. Only a saint could have resisted, and unfortunately there were few juvenile saints in our town. To the doctor's further disadvantage, he could not run fast. He tried. Leaving his splendid hat in the street where it had been knocked by the first direct hit, he would race after us, his elbows pumping up and down, his small, fashionable feet twinkling, his voice squeaking like a chicken's.

He was particularly vulnerable in neighborhoods graced by high, unpainted board fences full of splinters. These fences, lined up in shabby gray ranks along muddy alleys, were an architectural hallmark of our town in those days. Dr. Young was at least twelve inches too short to get a leg over one of them, so any fairly agile boy's escape was easy.

It was with deep regret that we heard of the acid editorial in the *Evening News*, expressing contentment over the fact that after two years the doctor had pulled up stakes. He had "shaken the dust of our fair city off his patent leathers," was the way Editor Jesse Austin Greene put it, and "gone to greener pastures."

"Their loss," he concluded, "is our gain."

Our neighborhood, on the ragged edge of a region that today would be considered ripe for urban renewal, sheltered a number of illustrious citizens. One of the first that I remember was the elderly gentleman known simply to us children as "Old Man." It never occurred to us that he might have a name, but definitely he had no home. We knew that some snowy nights he slept in the shed back of Mrs. Welsh's house across our alley and that Mrs. Welsh, a kindly lady, gave him a well-worn pink comforter with yellow roses on it. What really endeared him to us was the fact that he was the only person of our acquaintance we ever had seen pushed, screaming, kicking and biting, into a patrol wagon.

Old Man had the habit of standing outside our back fence in his shabby, unbuttoned overcoat and conversing in a loud voice with anyone at hand, and if no one were at hand he conversed affably anyhow. We never could quite understand what he said, but he paid attention to us and therefore we liked him. But one afternoon he got into the back yard and fell down and rolled in the snow and some heartless soul called the police. We blamed Miss Amelia, who worked for us. She never had understood our affection for the old gentleman in the alley, and she denied the allegation.

The Old Man won our further allegiance that day with a performance that ranked with Teddy Roosevelt's charge up San Juan Hill. He didn't want to get into the patrol wagon, and he said so. Officer Frank Chevron did not seem to understand him. So he gathered the Old Man by the seat of his pants and the back of his dirty coat and pushed.

Then it was that our hero tried to bite Officer Chevron, which was an error in both tactics and strategy. Officer Chevron weighed two-hundred-sixty pounds and had large, capable hands. When he put his heart into inserting a male-factor into the patrol wagon, it was one of the sights of the town. This time the vocal accompaniment furnished by his victim enhanced the drama. For years I could not think of

Officer Chevron without remembering bitterly that he not only pushed the Old Man, very rudely, into the patrol wagon, but also kicked him in the seat of the pants.

There was no real shock connected with this event. It was just something that happened. But shock *was* felt the summer night Alice, our pretty little colored help—people never had "servants," just "help"—was shot full of holes at our front gate in Clinton Street by what the *Evening Sentinel* called a "distraught suitor." My window was open. Angry voices had awakened me and I was hanging out the window, with the arc light on the corner making dappled shadows of maple trees on the grass, when the shooting began.

I rushed to my mother, who was reading *Littell's Living Age* in bed. Calm as always, she went downstairs to the telephone to call the police, then told me to stay indoors. She did not mention the window, so I went back to it.

Detective Charley Rulo arrived first, pumping his bicycle furiously. He was not as big a man as Officer Chevron, but he had pumped hard and he was panting as he ran to the gate with a cigar in one hand, a pistol in the other. He took charge of the emergency, and we had a great deal to tell other lads who never had been honored by a visit from a "distraught suitor."

After Old Man had left us, a black-browed character who worked for a trucking company became our personal devil. He was "The-Man-Who-Beat-Horses," and we hated him with all our juvenile might, which was considerable. When the law finally overtook him for burning down the trucking company office, we always felt that all the horses in the trucking barn had a good laugh.

Then there was Dr. Jones, a colored gentleman who "hung out" at my uncle's drug store. Dr. Jones was a corn doctor who claimed no medical school and performed his surgery with an old-fashioned straight razor on the corns, calluses and bunions of the working classes. But in our wide young eyes he was just as much a doctor as Dr. Young, or even Dr. Porter or Dr. Deming, who saw us through chicken pox and measles. We were fond of Dr. Jones and deeply hurt at what happened to him. One night he discovered that his wife—who wasn't really his wife, it turned out—had been "unfaithful" and he operated on her thoroughly with his sharp razor. It was the first time I ever heard the word "dissected."

There also was Mrs. Murkheiser, who lived in a small, not too neat house in Montgomery Street. She was an angular woman with a tight bun of hair on the top of her head and no sense of humor, whose husband worked as a molder in one of the foundries. Once, when I had successfully given her oldest offspring a bloody nose, she surprised my unguarded rear and yanked me home by an ear, telling my mother that I was the worst boy that ever walked on shoe leather, which even then I thought was a pretty way of putting it.

I managed to get along nicely with most of the lads in the neighborhood. They came chiefly from small, sooty houses in Holman and Montgomery Streets and the alleys that lay between. These houses often had no plumbing, not enough heat, and windows patched with the cardboard backs of school writing tablets. They smelled of boiling cabbage and Mail Pouch tobacco. The reading matter therein usually consisted of the Holy Bible with gilt edging or a Socialist weekly journal, or both if the family happened to be broad-minded, displayed on an ornate black-walnut parlor table with one weak leg, kept erect by a chunk of stovewood or a brick.

In these homes, full of poverty and pitchfork political philosophy, I was frequently exposed to fundamentalism, nihilism, solid Republicanism, Roman Catholicism and the theories of the Rev. Dwight L. Moody—whose golden voice and homey manner made his words sound more reasonable and respectable than they looked on the printed page—and always to talk of the far-fetched dreams of a nation blessed by social security as advocated by Mr. Eugene V. Debs.

These glory days of youth allowed any agile eight- or ten-year-old to lead a fascinating double life, enjoying the fruits of both his worlds. In a town of forty thousand, even a dirty-faced young hoodlum could associate with esteemed community leaders or with ladies and gentlemen just out of jail and about to go back. He could sit quietly in a corner, listening respectfully to the Hoosier authors and poets who visited his mother, or just as quietly in the Reverend Dr. Moffat's study reading the old bound volumes of *The Youth's Companion*, and within the hour he could heave a brick through the frosted glass in the front door of Mrs. Dawson's house on East Berry Street.

Of course he would justify the heathenish act by his knowledge that she was mean to cats and dogs and also objected to boys climbing trees. She liked birds, and the boys, she said, were trying to rob the nests. We were not. It was just that the buckeye trees across the sidewalk from her house were so full of foliage that they made a safe hiding place for half a dozen young fellows to enjoy a sport that Bill Moffat's uncle inadvertently had imported.

When the uncle came home from China, where he had been a missionary among unbelievers, he brought a pocketful of coins with square holes in them for his young admirers. We weren't so sheltered that we had not heard of the old pocketbook trick. So we tied two or three coins together on a long string, and on summer evenings in a tree across from Mrs. Dawson's house waited for our victims.

Young love was in bloom along East Berry Street, and as couples in fond embrace slowly made their ecstatic way through the darkness beneath us, we would drop the coins on the end of the string to the sidewalk. They tinkled; romance was swiftly forgotten while lovers lit matches and crawled about hunting the nickels and dimes they imagined they themselves had dropped in their often athletic lovemaking. Of course we had quickly jerked up the string, and hanging in leafy darkness, enjoyed the sights.

Heathen money was never put to better use. But Mrs. Dawson watched from her window, and one night, still fussing about birds, she called the Humane Officer and he talked to our parents.

The statute of limitations permits me to disclose that it was I who hurled the brick the next day, with Bill Moffat the witness. So that it would not make too much noise, I wrapped it in newspapers first, threw it, and then Bill and I ran. Mrs.

Dawson had no telephone. She used the one down the block in the study of neighborly Dr. Moffat. His son Bill and I reached the parsonage ahead of her and sat innocently, even if a little out of breath, reading *The Youth's Companion,* all the time that she told the police on the phone the awful story about the brick. She exaggerated frightfully. It had been deep dusk at the moment of Bill's and my foray, and she could not possibly have recognized us, but certainly she did know it was not four strong men with pistols who had attacked her, just two small boys with one brick.

It was Officer Stevens who responded this time. He was a tall, slow-footed guardian of the law who strolled his beat, never quickening his pace even on cold February days. The department considered juveniles his specialty, and he usually was a reasonable man who believed in letting well enough alone. He always managed to be going past Seidel's pastry shop as the day's new batch of charlotte russe was placed on display in the front window, under pink mosquito netting in summer, bare in winter. Officer Stevens would drop in casually and come out with a piece of cake and cream, which he ate with satisfaction as he strolled on. It was darkly hinted that he never paid for the pastry.

He was an extremely thin man, despite his daily ration at Seidel's, and when he questioned a boy he had a peculiar habit of pulling at his long, thin mustaches, first one side, then the other. His idea of a thorough investigation was to ask a couple of questions in a pleasant tone of voice, and if one did not confess immediately, to stroll on, completely satisfied. This heartwarming example of Christian fellowship made him very much beloved by a generation of young scoundrels.

On the day of the brick incident, he may have searched diligently for the culprits elsewhere but he did not approach Dr. Moffat's, and when next he saw us on the street he merely spoke pleasantly, despite the hangdog looks we must have worn.

All boys owned back-yard shanties, either singly or in concert with their friends. They usually were built of bits and pieces of lumber discovered loose here and there and no questions asked, and the more pretentious of them had flattened tin cans for roofing.

Bill Moffat and I had created a very special one in the Moffat yard and even papered its interior against the cold with several thicknesses of *The Evening News*. Here we plotted our deeds of virtue, violence or valor. But one late afternoon in the early winter dusk, a trio of brothers from up the street, with whom we were having a misunderstanding on some weighty matter of ethics, slipped into the yard and deftly tore our shanty to pieces.

We heard the crash and rushed out into the dark to view the pitiful ruins. The scoundrels had fled. Of course, we knew at once who they were, and we pledged our honor to revenge the wrong instantly and with interest. If they had destroyed our shanty, we would do the same to theirs.

Dr. Moffat stored not only *The Youth's Companion* but hundreds of other magazines in the closet off his study. Sparing the *Companion*, we helped ourselves to *The Christian Century*, and stopping in the kitchen only long enough to snitch some matches, we eased out the back door unnoticed and raced down the alley. By the time we reached the home grounds of the villains, they had been called in for supper.

We tore and crumpled the magazines and stuffed them into all the corners of the enemy shanty, struck our matches and ran. We not only had reached the Moffat residence, but were washed and ready for our own suppers when we heard the bell on Number One Engine House begin to tap. The nearby sound of fire horses' hooves on Clay Street attracted even Dr. Moffat, who never was a fast-moving man, but when he saw the glow in the sky he quickened his pace almost to a run.

Bill and I hung back modestly. This time we would watch the conflagration from a distance. *The Christian Century* was non-incriminating ash by the time the firemen got into the ruin, and no one ever tore down our shanties again.

Virtue may be its own reward for pious adults, but for young fellows deeply injured by their neighbors, villainy also paid off.

12

HIGH ADVENTURE WITH
THE CRIMINAL CLASSES

I REGRET that I never met Mr. Marvin Kuhns. It was my bad luck, I am sure, for Mr. Kuhns was practicing his profession of horse thief when I was born and continued to practice it up to about my sixteenth year. Had I displayed a bit more spirit I might now be able to boast, "This is the hand that shook the hand of Marvin Kuhns."

On the east side of Calhoun Street in Fort Wayne, between Montgomery and Holman Streets, just south of Mr. Jones' Troy Steam Laundry, stood a plain-faced, two-story brick building called the Commercial Hotel. It never got into either the *Guide Michelin* or the *Hotel Redbook*, but it had a fame all its own that had nothing to do with comfortable beds or fine food. I used to eye it from all directions, curious but scared, remembering the tales I had been told of its earlier and more exciting life.

For it was there that the Philabaum Gang made its evil headquarters. Now before anyone picks up the telephone to call his lawyer, let me make it clear that these Philabaums were in no way related to or connected with anyone of that noble name living now in Indiana, Ohio, Alaska, Puerto Rico or anywhere else in the world. It just happened to be the title of a gang of aggressive and inspired horse thieves in which Mr. Kuhns originally was an apprentice.

Missouri had its Jesse James, London its Jack the Ripper, but they were rank amateurs compared with this Indiana boy from Churubusco who made good in a bad way. Mr. Kuhns was locked up in jail regularly and escaped regularly; and if one happened to be driving quietly along a country road in northern Indiana or Ohio, thinking pleasant thoughts, and discovered concentrations of angry farmers with shotguns at every crossroad, it meant that Marvin was out again and had stolen another horse.

Even my Grandfather Goshorn on occasion took his rifle and hurried out grimly to his farm west of town to spend the night guarding the poor steed that rattlesnakes later were to kill. Mr. Kuhns never did visit the farm. Before he had opportunity, he was riding a stolen horse on an Ohio road near the Indiana line when he died of an overdose of pistol shots from a deputy sheriff's Smith-and-Wesson thirty-eight.

He was buried in Wolf Lake cemetery not far from his birthplace, the Reverend Mr. Cole of Kendallville having been chosen, much against his will it was said, to conduct the service. He did it with rare delicacy, using quotations from the Book of Job, including the indisputable fact that, "Man born of a woman is of few days and full of trouble . . . he cometh forth like a flower, and is cut down." My mother said it must have been touching. The Northern Indiana Horse Thief Protective Association attended in a well-armed body, probably wanting to make doubly sure there had been no mistake in identification.

Mr. Kuhns was the earliest, but by no means the last bad man in my gallery. He shot more people than any of the others but was no more exciting. One rival killed only one person, but his method for disposing of the body gives him special prominence.

Fortunately, at least so far as these reminiscences are concerned, I have forgotten his name. But he held me in goose-pimple enthrallment for several weeks. Having been encouraged to read at an early age, I was a regular student of all local papers. That is how I discovered, in a copy of the *News* that Uncle Gustave brought home, the fascinating details of the man who stuffed little Annie's body down a well.

My mother, who, as it has been pointed out, preferred the *Evening Sentinel* to Uncle Gustave's *News* because it supported Mr. Bryan, gave as another reason her suspicion that the *News* found it too profitable to go on an occasional crime-reporting binge. It usually was difficult in our town to dredge up enough crime to make a binge, for we were stuffily respectable in most events that got into the papers. The juiciest happenings always seemed to occur in carriage-trade families connected either with members of the city council or with advertisers, who frowned, then as now, on seeing their names in the police-court news.

But poor little Annie didn't advertise or ride in a carriage, so in her case the *News* could go on a binge even bigger than usual.

I could hardly wait for Uncle Gustave to arrive each evening with the paper and with it would run to the cellar steps, where I gobbled up the latest chapter under the gas light. The villain in question lived in the small village of Wallen, some six or seven miles north of our town on the Grand Rapids and Indiana Railroad, and if my memory is as clear as I hope it is, and the chalk-plate drawings in the *Evening News* were fairly accurate, he wore what among ladies would have been called a pompadour, and a long, dark mustache big enough to hide a Hohner harmonica.

One reason for my goose-pimple enthrallment was the *News'* disclosure that several weeks after little Annie disappeared and the hue and cry turned up no clue to her whereabouts, her bereaved family tasted something peculiar in the well water, and, investigating, found all that remained of little Annie.

The villain from Wallen was suspected, questioned and "forced to confess," according to the *News,* whose editor had never heard the charges that policemen sometimes are careless about a citizen's civil rights.

Civil rights or no, the wicked man told the whole story,

which the *News* repeated down to the last soul-shattering detail, and my hair for days stood erect and rebuffed all efforts of comb and brush. Sheriff Melshing had "incarcerated" the villain, the paper said. Here was another word full of hidden suggestions that sent me racing to the works of Mr. Noah Webster. It was disappointing to discover that it meant only that Sheriff Melshing had locked him up, all in one piece, in the Allen County Jail.

That was where the culprit was sitting when my mother discovered what I was reading and commanded Uncle Gustave to leave the *News* at the bank or throw it away before he came into the house. This was inconvenient, since it made it necessary for me to go down to Elliott Crosby's house near Chestnut Street to read the paper his father didn't have to throw away. Elliott had not had my advantages, though he was a year older than I and just as fascinated as I by the goings-on in Wallen, but he couldn't read and had to wait for me each day to bring him up to date.

Some time later, when reading newspapers had become a less secret habit, I discovered that the man from Wallen who had been nasty to little Annie had "paid the supreme penalty," but that he first had presented his soul to his Maker, so had few worries about the hereafter. I always did wonder what little Annie's family had done about that well. The newspaper never said.

The first fiend-in-human-form I knew personally was a gentleman whose name definitely was not Benny Kaviski, but for reasons of family pride and the peculiar way juries have of finding against anyone who puts pencil to paper to record the facts, he must remain Mr. Kaviski.

He was a smallish man with a long dark crinkly beard and the serene expression of an Old Testament prophet, who spoke softly in an accent usually incomprehensible to me, and had the gentle, limpid eyes of an elderly collie dog. He wore his hair down around his collar and covered most of it with a big black fedora hat, deeply creased fore and aft.

Mr. Kaviski ran a little tailor shop, but most of his tailoring was concerned with sewing patches on pants and in cleaning suits. "Dry cleaning," he called it, and it consisted of swishing a garment around in a tub of benzine, brushing it thoroughly with a genuine hog-bristle brush and hanging it in the back window to dry. After that he pressed it, and all the owner needed to do after he got the garment home was hang it in the back yard for days to try to get rid of the benzine odor, usually without great success.

About the same time Mr. Kaviski ran afoul of the law, another gentleman of our acquaintance also got himself into serious trouble. Let's call him Jim Butts. It was in reference to Mr. Butts that I first met the word "firebug." In four or five glorious hours that evening, he set eleven fires, most of them highly successful, in stables, a schoolhouse, an undertaking parlor and the back room of Mr. Ankenbruck's saloon.

Mr. Kaviski's crime was quite different. It caused similar public consternation, but in contrast to Mr. Butts's, reactions were either numbing shock or rollicking amusement. For he was known briefly by the entire town as "The Man Who Stole The Bible."

Benny was an ardent member of a small, poverty-ridden Orthodox synagogue on Clinton Street near Holman, less than two blocks away from our house. We used to see Benny, who lived in an ancient three-story brick on Lewis Street, on his way to services each Saturday morning. He walked with his thin white hands folded across his lean middle, and his black suit was neatly brushed, black hat firmly set upon his head, black beard combed, black eyes turned inward in Sabbath contemplation.

His piety was so manifest no one would have been either startled or surprised had he suddenly sprouted a halo. Perhaps it was this kinship with divinity that kept bad little boys from tossing rocks at him from the roof of the old coach house at the end of our lot.

After Benny was arrested, the newspapers explained in some detail that the congregation to which he belonged had been torn by one of those cataclysms that can center only in a violent theological misunderstanding. There had been dissatisfaction with the rabbi, a gentleman in a long black robe with

black rope sash and a hat of immense proportions, who was
Benny Kaviski's dear friend. The black beard of this gentleman of the cloth was so vast and overwhelming it made poor
Benny's amply whiskered chin look positively naked, but that
did not seem in any way to reduce Benny's affection for him.

The congregation, which numbered something under a hundred, after soul searching and loud discussion in which Benny
played a noisy part, had sacked his friend from his eight-
hundred-dollar-a-year post and employed a new rabbi from
out of town. This Saturday morning was to be the newcomer's
first sermon.

I am not skilled enough in theology, even after all these
years, to understand just what the tenets of the congregation
were, but it seems that in order to hold the services, it was
necessary to have the Talmud in the edifice. Not any Talmud,
but a very special one. So on Friday night, after locking up his
tailor shop, Benny slipped through dark alleys—and all alleys
in our neighborhood were dark—and found his way to the
synagogue. By prying open a window, he got in. With the
sacred Talmud under his arm, he crawled out; he concealed
the volume under a great pile of shingles in Mr. Ed Gilmartin's lumber yard. If there were no Talmud, no new rabbi
could preach. It was as simple as that.

The congregation, arriving to do honor to the new leader,
was horrified at the desecration and began to cast about for
the guilty party. Of course saintly Benny was marked from the
start. Not only did he refuse to join in the hue and cry, he
refused even to look shocked. So the police arrived and took
him to the city lockup on Barr Street, where he confessed his
sins. Patrolmen Peter Junk and Charley Spillner rescued the
Talmud from the lumber yard.

Benny's wickedness fascinated us. The *Journal-Gazette* even
ran a scorching editorial against "The Man Who Stole The
Bible." Colonel Andy Moynihan, who wrote it, referred to the
crime as "heinous." After Benny got out of jail, he used to
walk, still meekly, past our house on his way to his shop, but
now we all gave him a wide berth. There was something just a
little too wicked to be forgiven about a man who could steal a

Bible, even a Bible that for some reason bore the name of Talmud.

Jim Butts, in contrast to meek Mr. Kaviski, was a big, bluff, hearty man, a little on the soft side mentally, who made his living as a handyman around a saloon. The Saturday night he put on his big act, we were living in the house on Barr Street. It had been a hot, sunny, windless afternoon, dry and dispiriting as early July so often is in Indiana.

There had been little for us to do all day. Phenomenal Francis, the tape-worm impresario, had struck the tents of his medicine show on Helmke's lot, behind the billboards at the corner of Calhoun and Montgomery Streets, and taken his bottles and entertainers elsewhere. Harold Warner, who lived across Barr Street from us, had gone with his parents to Rome City for a week on Sylvan Lake. Kurt Feiertag from across Lewis Street was having to practice his violin. The Munkheiser boys up Montgomery Street were in a friendly mood for once, so there was no rock heaving.

The whole day had been uneventful, except that a young bird had fallen out of its nest in one of the elm trees and broken its neck. My brothers Don and little Gus and sister Dorothy buried all baby birds out behind the house close to the lilac hedge, but for some reason the funeral was always held on the front walk. It was around seven o'clock and I was watching my sister Dorothy and Luella Feiertag getting ready for these obsequies when the real excitement began. The bell on Number One Engine House on East Main Street rapped out an alarm. It tapped one-two-one, which was Box 121 out in front of its own door. When an alarm came in by telephone or someone galloped up to the station in his buggy to report a conflagration, Mr. Peggy Thieme always sounded the number of the box close at hand.

Mr. Thieme was a friend of every boy in town, willing to take anyone back to the stalls to pat the three-horse engine hitch, Sam, Pete and Max, on their soft pink noses. He had lost a leg at a fire years before. Everyone else I knew who had to get along with one leg or arm had been crippled as a result of running to catch one of the new electric cars, forgetting that unlike the horse cars, they could make up to ten or twelve miles an hour and the runner could fall under the wheels.

But Peggy's leg was crushed at a blaze on Columbia Street, and because his injury was sustained on duty, he held his job. Since he was unable to carry hose, climb ladders or even to drive a rig—its driver needed a good foot for the bell, the other for the wheel brake—he had been assigned to a telephone watch at Number One where the alarms came in.

Our firemen put in seven-day weeks and twenty-four-hour days, with time out to go home for dinner and supper, if they lived within the block, which most of them did. Occasionally one of them, hearing the bell, would charge back with his mouth full of meat and potatoes. They had two days off every month and a week's summer vacation. It was a fine job, paying forty-five dollars a week, and if you were lucky and of the proper political complexion, you could become a lieutenant or a captain after the votes were counted, and last year's lieutenants or captains became firemen in the ranks. Strangely, much the same unprofessional system is in vogue in the city today.

The bell had hardly finished tolling off 1-2-1 this evening when it started to ring again, this time tapping off the box from Number Three Engine House on West Washington; then a call from the far east side from Engine Four, and after only a brief pause, another across the railroad track from Engine and Ladder Truck Two.

Anyone who didn't know the locations of these numbered boxes had only to turn to the back page of the Home Telephone Book where they were listed. Most small boys did not need the book, however. They might have trouble with simple arithmetic and the geography of North America, but they knew the exact location of each of the eighty-seven fire-alarm boxes in the town and needed only to hear the number to start to run in the right direction.

This particular evening as the bell tolled out the fateful combinations, I stopped each time to pant and listen, then turned and headed for the latest. I was running west on

Douglas Avenue when Box 67 banged in and I swung around
again and put on more speed.

Box 67 was at the corner of Barr and Madison Streets, just
half a block from our house. By the time I reached the corner,
I could see smoke east on Madison. It came from a barn on
the back of a lot with a small yellow-brick house with colored
glass artistry across the top of its parlor windows.

Herr Professor Schroeder of St. Paul's *Evangelische Schule*
lived just two doors from the burning barn. By the time I
climbed two board fences and ran across three back yards, the
Herr Professor and several neighbors had rescued two horses
from the blaze and were trying to push a recalcitrant cow
through a grape arbor to get her to safety. They succeeded,
leaving nothing inside but a sleigh. Two big boys, all of twelve
or fifteen years old, were already there. The sleigh was worth
saving, too, we thought, an elegant cutter with curved dashboard and tasseled whip, so together we hauled it out.

"I saw him!" a shrill woman was telling Herr Professor
Schroeder. "I saw him run out! Out that door! Right there! A
firebug!"

Here was another word I never had heard before, and my
immediate mental picture was of a huge insect, running fast
and trailing flame. Then I realized that "firebug" was a figure
of speech. It was a man, probably wearing a black cloak and
having a black hat pulled down over his eyes. He had a
firebrand in his skinny hand and was slipping from doorway to
doorway.

Before my imagination could go on from there, the first
engine arrived. It came from Number Four out on Maumee
Avenue. Right behind it, Chief Henry Hilbrecht raced into
sight. He was a big, jovial, florid man with a pair of white
mustaches. When you passed him on the street he gave off a
pleasant aroma of good beer, walked slowly and even had
time to say "Good morning" to small boys.

On his way to a fire, however, he was far from slow. He
leaned forward across the dashboard of his light "buggy," as
chiefs' cars are called everywhere, even in this automotive age,

and drove fast and dramatically. His broad-chested dapple-gray horse had learned to "mind the bell." When the chief kicked it fast, the horse sprinted; when the bell tempo was slower, the horse took up a more leisurely gait.

Most of Chief Hilbrecht's time not devoted to battling fires, which like good murders ordinarily were rather few in Fort Wayne, he spent in the cool and beery comfort of Strodel's East Main Street Saloon, a scant half-block from Number One. Much of the day he kept his buggy outside the place—every saloon was a "place" in those days—and needed only to rush out, wiping the beer from his great white mustache, and be off to the blaze.

This night the ladder truck from Number One and the hose wagon and chemical rig with its burnished brass tanks from Number Three were right behind the chief.

For the next few hours there was nothing dull about the streets of our town. Dignified citizens who had not run a step since the night President Garfield was assassinated charged up and down the sidewalks, as many running north as ran south. Fire engines met and passed one another answering alarms. The hose-cart team from Number Three wore particularly pained, confused expressions after the fourth alarm in twenty minutes. By that time the chief's big gray was in a steaming lather and the police patrol wagon that always followed the fire apparatus, with Driver Cy Andrews handling the team of chestnuts on the tongue, practically met itself coming back as it raced from one spot to another.

Nothing quite like that sultry night ever, before or after, happened in Fort Wayne. There could be riots in New York, earthquakes in San Francisco, a World's Fair in St. Louis, but Fort Wayne for one glorious and frantic evening had Jim Butts the Firebug and a chorus of crackling blazes, clattering hooves and ringing bells.

Even Officer Stevens, known for his leisurely tempo, somewhere got a bicycle and scorched up and down streets. Like every other boy, I tried to attend all the conflagrations, and while racing from a blaze behind Mr. Lepper's drug store on West Jefferson Street and one near Mr. Bass's car-wheel works on Hanna, I inadvertently ran straight past our house. It was a tactical error. I could have made just as good time by way of Holman Street and would not have had to answer any questions.

My mother had come out of the double iron gates and was standing on the corner, talking to Mrs. Center across the way. Mrs. Center usually took her leisure in summer sitting in her front door, with her knees propping open the screen, but tonight she, too, had gone to the corner to see in all directions.

"The firebug's setting fire to barns!" I panted. "Everybody's saving horses! Dozens of barns . . ."

Number One's bell began to ring again.

"Barns?" my mother repeated. "Are you sure? Setting fire to barns?" She started to walk fast, then to run northward in Barr. "Come with me," she shouted.

There was a new fire on Wallace Street that I should have attended, but my mother did not stop to listen. I would come with her immediately. She was a large woman who found it difficult and inconvenient ever to sprint, but that night she sprinted. Straight down Barr to Berry, east on Berry to the rather ornate brick and stone home of her friend Miss Louise Carnahan.

Miss Carnahan owned a beautiful carriage horse named Daisy who lived in a fancy brick stable at the foot of the Carnahan lot. We arrived to find Louise and her brother Bob and their mother all looking west in Berry Street, where a new blaze had broken out.

"He's burning horses!" my mother cried. "We must save Daisy!"

So there is where I spent the remainder of an eventful evening. My mother with a buggy whip and Louise with a golf club guarded the barn door, not permitting me to venture even as far as the Clay Street crossing when the ladder truck rolled that way. Not until the news arrived belatedly that Detectives Pete Cooling and Charley Rulo had apprehended the scoundrel and that he was safe in jail did our vigil end.

But when we discovered that our dear friend Jim Butts, who was not too grown-up or high and mighty to pause sometimes and play a game with juveniles, had been arrested and had confessed, we were heartbroken. To us, Jim didn't look like a firebug. He just looked like Jim Butts. And he had a thoroughly understandable and logical reason for setting his fires. He only wanted to see the horses run.

In later years when I heard Chicagoans talking of their pet gangster, Al Capone, I felt sorry for them. Few had seen him in the flesh, had never known him the way we knew Jim Butts. When Jim Butts got back from serving his time in the state penitentiary, he became a good citizen. Well, not exactly that. But he never set any more barns on fire and he remained reasonably sober and got terribly fat over the years. Even though, I suppose, in comparison with his big night, they were very dull years.

13

___

CURTAIN CALLS

THE PENNSYLVANIA RAILROAD and its pioneering predecessor, the Pittsburgh, Fort Wayne and Chicago, made ours a "good theatre town." That was in the gilded age for which romantic old actors still weep into their tea, remembering, not unhappily, the hard, weary, often hungry theatrical life called "the road."

Fort Wayne was a railroad division point where all trains halted in their steamy races between New York and Chicago. Broadway shows sped west, with brief layovers in Philadelphia, Pittsburgh, sometimes Harrisburg and other large Main Line towns, then on to Fort Wayne. Or plays that later became Broadway hits opened in Chicago at the Iroquois, McVickers and Great Northern, names to turn any stage-struck young head. If critics in the *Record Herald* or the *Inter-Ocean* were kind, the Chicago companies started east triumphantly. If reviews were frightful, then frenzied managers, frantic playwrights and imperious stars screamed at one another, sewed up holes in plots, rewrote dialogue and tried out revised efforts on small-town dogs. Among spots where they stopped hopefully a night or two was Mr. Frank Stouder's Temple Theatre and Opera House, just six blocks down the street from our gate.

When troupes were due at the Pennsy depot, boys lay in wait on the plank platform in front of Mr. McKinnie's Railroad Hotel and Eating House, where, everyone knew, white linen tablecloths were changed after every meal. The station, across the tracks from the Wabash, was two stories high in its central section, supporting the Hotel; and by design or accident, the Limiteds always halted with sleeping-car steps directly opposite the inviting door of the Eating House.

Boys, congregating at the depot to sniff the hot oily smell of axle boxes and listen to steam locomotives' impatient panting, watched the rich people picking their way through cinders, the men with derby hats and big gold watch chains, the women with "wasp waists," which Editor Jesse Austin Greene of the *News* for some reason deplored in print, and on their hats plumes slightly smaller than the locomotive driving wheel. Regardless of what any of them wore, they all carried good appetites. The world was less demented than it is now, so who would think it strange that those ultra-modern trains called "flyers," after spurts of sixty-five miles an hour, idled for a pleasant twenty minutes for noon dinner, or supper any time between five and seven o'clock?

Big, coal-black John Moten, a waiter who gave service-with-a-grin, was a friend of all boys. We admired the way he ran the length of the train, banging out the happy news that soup was on, with a wooden spoon on a battered copper tray. It was a mark of juvenile social distinction to be Mr. Moten's friend, like knowing the governor or sheriff. Mr. Moten rewarded friendship with bits of hot pastry or small chunks of cake. Having a big heart, if Mr. McKinnie were not looking, he extended his generosity to those unfortunates that unkind people called "hoboes," who lounged in muddy Railroad Avenue, waiting for Mr. McKinnie to make his daily trip to the bank. They annoyed Mr. McKinnie. But after he left, they sometimes found on the back step dainties hardly hurt at all by having been scraped off a diner's plate.

Passenger conductors always gulped their modest meals, usually a sandwich with three slices of ham plus a cup of well-creamed coffee, all for a dime, which was just half the high

price regular customers paid. The conductors then stood help-
fully in the restaurant door, blue caps politely tucked under
their arms, gold watches in hand, courteously announcing how
much time remained, at five-minute intervals, then at the two-
minute mark while passengers swallowed their apple pie.
Finally, with thirty seconds left, came the stern, "All aboard,
folks. Sorry, folks, all aboard." People may not have lived as
long in those tranquil times, but they lived better.

Mr. Bide Barnett, a pleasant, chunky man in a plaid cap,
sent horse-drawn omnibuses to meet all trains. They carried
eight passengers inside, baggage on top, and sometimes an
extra man gripping the brass handrails and living dangerously
on the back step. Mr. Barnett also had two-horse hacks to take
traveling salesmen and well-to-do strangers to the Aveline
House, the less well-to-do to the Randall or the Wayne. Politicians, including the governor, stayed at the Randall, paying
two and a half dollars a day for three meals and bed.

Most other arriving travelers, such as famous members of
Central League ball teams from South Bend, Grand Rapids or
Dayton, walked to the Rich Hotel carrying their bags. It was
only four short blocks and two-men-in-a-bed cost fifty cents a
night; flannel cakes, ham and two eggs for breakfast were
twenty cents—light subsistence for a fellow supposed to hit
the ball over the fence into Clinton Street, but good actors
those days got considerably better pay than good ball players.

With important stage folk due, Mr. Barnett took special
pains. Hacks were clean and polished, hubs and springs
greased against unseemly squeaks, horses well curried. And he
had one driver with a sense of "theatre," who could capture
easily all illustrious dramatic personae. Mr. Cy Fike, hearse
driver at most of Undertaker Jim Peltier's more majestic
funerals, did for Mr. Barnett what today is called moon-
lighting.

A fair actor himself, Mr. Fike once had dissolved in sobs at
the funeral of a man he detested when he realized the widow
was looking at him. Not only a touching tragedian, he played
lighter roles with verve. To greet troupers, his costume consisted of a pilfered flower on the lapel of a rusty, swallow-

tailed coat, and a slightly faded top hat with a motheaten red
turkey feather stuck rakishly in the band. He always removed
the feather for funerals. Instead of a buggy whip to prod the
team, he carried only a short crop, proof to any soft-hearted
lady that he was kind to animals. As possible customers
approached, Mr. Fike removed his hat with a fine Elizabethan
gesture and laid it on his forearm. Quickly recognizing one of
their own, troupers naturally headed toward his shining hack
and a Sir Walter Raleigh welcome. They were philanthropic
tippers, he said.

Boys in school might confuse Richard the Lion-Hearted with
Poor Richard of Philadelphia, but watching theatrical troupes
get off the train, they never confused Mr. Richard Mansfield
with anyone. He played Beau Brummell, on stage and off.
Swinging down the step of the Pullman Palace Car, he did not
allow weather or clock to keep him from removing his big,
furry fedora hat to the first woman he saw, showing bright
teeth and curly hair, bowing from the waist and looking taller
than he really was.

I knew that Christopher Marlowe wrote a poem about melodious birds and madrigals because my mother liked to quote
it, but I had a much more personal feeling about that other
magnificent Marlowe, the lovely Miss Julia. Once she spoke to
me and I felt a sensation that came to me only once more in
my life, when Winston Churchill asked me a logistics question
at a staff meeting in World War II. Miss Marlowe not only
spoke; she smiled, not at my dirty bare feet, but my dirty
enraptured face. With no close competitor at all, she was the
prettiest lady ever to step down daintily from an observation
car, and when in her magnificent ermine robe she appeared as
Mary Tudor in *When Knighthood Was in Flower,* nobody
thought that the seats were too expensive. They were a dollar
for opening week and most tickets until then had cost only
twenty-five cents.

Charles Major, the author-lawyer from Shelbyville whose
characters jousted all over Europe in *When Knighthood Was
in Flower,* one might have expected to come to town in casque
and chain armor, or at least with a feather in his cap. But he

did not. Instead, the day I saw him walking into Pellins' and Polster's Drug Store, he had a slightly dusty, mousy air. He wore a plain pepper-and-salt suit just like everybody else, and with enough money to buy all the hats he needed, he was wearing a black derby that looked too small. He carried an ordinary bundle wrapped in newspapers, and the pockets of his unpressed pants bulged out, with what one could imagine were royalties from his plays. I had read *Knighthood*. There was nothing dusty or mousy about it.

The exotic denizens of Broadway and Herald Square—both of which recently had given up gas light in favor of Mr. Edison's dangerous electric bulbs—usually arrived on Eastbound 22 or Westbound 23, which Ticket Agent John Ross called "The-Manhattan-Limited-World's-Fastest-and-Best-Train," all one proud word. Hack drivers and boys always knew just which hour of which day, preferably a Saturday, to get to the station. Advance men with posters had plastered the town, distributed quarter-sheets and window cards in saloons and barber shops and empty store buildings. The pictures were often flattering, but at least they gave an approximate idea of what to expect, and in our town all of them, actors, managers, prop men, grips, playwrights like Mr. Major or Mr. Booth Tarkington were "Important People," every inch as respectable as doctors, judges, or the Herr Professors at Concordia College. And much more exciting. They traveled with more style and more luggage.

Sometimes, if the production were lavish, they carried their own baggage cars, jammed with big "theatrical trunks" larger and heavier than the average eight-lid kitchen stove, long rolls of backdrops, wing flats, drop flies and crates of other special scenery and props, all dusted beautifully with a fine coat of cinders. If seeing Mr. Wallace's circus from Peru unload was a good day's adventure, getting to the station in time to watch a big company arrive was almost as worthwhile. A pretty young girl named Blanche Bates, starring in *Under Two Flags*, was in one of the troupes that arrived with its own baggage car. But the outfit that topped all others was General Lew Wallace's *Ben Hur*.

The cast of the *Ben Hur* road company was considerably smaller, I believe, than the original four hundred that packed the New York stage. The play had been crisscrossing the country for many years by now. Half the people in our town were among the millions who saw it—twenty million was one count, but this was before the days of computers, so who knows? And half as many, at least, had read the Palestine story. It was an achievement to have a book translated into one foreign language, but *Ben Hur* not only had been published in every language in Europe including the Russian, but also in Japanese and Arabic.

General Wallace was an authentic Hoosier hero, just as much as General Anthony Wayne had been, with more adventure in his life than most boys ever dreamed of. He had been a Mexican War lieutenant, had done a cloak-and-dagger job in Mexico and the Texas Republic, had raised a regiment for the Civil War, and either saved Grant's reputation at Shiloh and Pittsburg Landing or ruined it, my father said. Both stories persisted. Sometime in between, he had captained a Zouave troop that did foot drills at double time in Algerian uniforms, with baggy pants and red fezes, like the one that performed with Buffalo Bill and Grandfather Goshorn wondered why.

The Zouaves were a special outfit in people's regard, not only because their uniforms set all the girls' hearts beating double time—this was Uncle Gustave's reasoning—but chiefly, and the story grew with every G.A.R. encampment, because of the fact that before the General took his gorgeous Zouaves to the Civil War, he had marched them to the State House in Indianapolis and made them kneel and swear by all that was holy to atone for Indiana's defeat at Buena Vista in the Mexican War. I always regretted that no one in my family, not even an in-law or cousin-third-removed, had been a Zouave. It put me to a disadvantage with several boys.

The General came up to Fort Wayne occasionally in his last years, usually to speak at a patriotic ceremony. He was still practicing law in Crawfordsville, still a Republican bigwig. Disappointingly, he never wore his splendid uniform on these visits, not even any Algerian pants. But he walked very straight, with his big head thrown back, making his white beard stick straight out in front.

Someone had told my friend Bill Moffatt and me that Jesus Christ might appear in person in *Ben Hur,* and I passed the fact on to my younger brothers and sister. None of us really believed it. In fact, Bill's Presbyterian preacher father called the idea "blasphemous," but just the same we were disappointed to see only a shaft of light instead of the Hero. It was one of Mr. Edison's first big dazzlers, though, and the chariots and horses were genuine enough and the villain got his comeuppance under thundering hooves. Pontius Pilate, the Wandering Jew, all the assorted Greeks, Egyptains, Arabs, Romans and Christian saints were in costumes such as never had been imagined.

We watched the cars unpack, watched the show, watched the reloading and hoped the whole outfit—horses, chariots, treadmill and people—would come again next week.

Except for summer activities in a park north of town, the only theatre was the Temple, in the Masonic Building on Clinton Street. There had been earlier opera houses. Grandfather Goshorn liked to tell about the one where the management helped ticket sales by serving free beer at intermissions; another had a bathhouse on the first floor—hot, cold or a shower for ten cents, including towels. The Temple was a pretentious structure of pressed red brick and sandstone with marble pillars at the entrance, its original plans so ambitious that after the builders had finished the first story—this, too, from my builder grandfather—there was a delay of several years while the Masons raised money to finish it and decorate their lodge rooms on the third floor. When it was ready, it was dedicated with a flourish, with a series of four grand operas for which richer townspeople, and some like Grandfather not so rich, paid ten dollars for the season, just to help culture and the Masonic Lodge.

The Temple could accommodate around five hundred and fifty persons, with two boxes on each side of the main floor and two on each side of the balcony level, from which, by stretching, one could see at least half of the stage. Ladies with ostrich plumes sat in these boxes. The first ten or twelve rows were in the pit, and a little above it and to the rear was the dress circle, with the finest seats. They were upholstered in a rich maroon velvet, and the shoulder-high partition that ran around the back of the lower floor also was covered with it, so if a boy without a ticket were allowed in to watch the play, he could rest his elbows on the velvet and be fairly comfortable.

Temple Theatre's manager, Frank Stouder, was my family's good friend; my father and he once had sung in the same quartet. His brother, Jake, who was forced by economics to spend part of his time unhappily running a hardware store, was my mother's friend, for he was a local historian. So they both became my mentors, and Frank, appreciating a boy's fascination with drama, would open the stage door and let me slip down the iron stairway at his well-shined heels, to a glamorous, undressed region below the stage.

Dusty, airless, badly lighted, it had a few broken chairs, messages pinned to a board, and around shabby walls, six or seven closed doors. They led to dressing rooms, I discovered; the first one opposite the stair, with the faded gilt star on it, belonged to the star in that night's play.

The "green room," people called this area—a place dingy and romantic at the same time, with a sweet, never-to-be-forgotten smell made up of grease paint, dust, sweat, tobacco, second-hand air, someone's left-over lunch, but chiefly grease paint.

Companies came for one-night stands, two nights, three, maybe six. But in any case, theatres remained decently dark on Sundays, so tired troupers could enjoy quiet Sabbaths. Sometimes some of them dined at our table, enjoying particularly the dessert that my mother, a good cook, called "French pudding," probably because she larded it generously with imported cognac we could not afford.

Some of the guests no doubt enjoyed our roof because it meant saving two dollars, the price of a night's lodging at the Aveline House. The hotel dated back only to the Civil War, but the name was one of Fort Wayne's oldest. The first Aveline had arrived in our parts so early that he had to be satisfied with a civil marriage service, the nearest priest being a hundred and thirty horseback miles away.

One show business guest who stayed with us on several exciting occasions was an old family friend whose real name, we children knew, even if less fortunate persons did not, was Mr. Walter T. Best. No one called him that. He was famous around the world as "E. Maro, Prince of Magic, Prestidigitator Extraordinary and Successor to Cagliostro." One only had to watch him closely, on stage or off, to realize that he could do anything—really anything—and what was more, he was generous with his secrets. He showed us how to palm a billiard ball and hide a silver dollar between our fingers.

Then came a tragic morning. The night before on the stage, I had watched Mr. Best, or Mr. Maro if you prefer, take a hand saw and cut his pretty wife, Allie, right in two, say "Presto Chango" in a French accent, and transform her into a screaming white cockatoo, and the cockatoo back to a smiling, whole, living, breathing Allie.

Next morning I was on my way along the hall to our bathroom when the Maro door opened and he stepped out. I always had admired his smoothly parted, slightly curly light-brown hair and wondered how one made hair so obedient. This morning as I looked up at him, horror overwhelmed me. His head was naked! No lock or curl, only white, bare skin. And in his hand he held his neatly parted hair as casually as if it had been a washcloth. I had never even heard of a wig.

"Good morning," he said cordially, but I could not answer, could only flee. I remembered Miss Murphy's family that had been scalped, but Maro never had mentioned Indians or the Wild West. I avoided him until he went to catch the ten o'clock train, and looking down from my window could see his hair all in place as he waved his hat. After that experience —traumatic, if you will—I never again could be sure of anyone or anything.

A distinguished actor who often used our spare room was Mr. Elias Day. Later he operated a successful school of acting in Chicago and many a Broadway or Hollywood star owed much to him. Late evenings in our living room he entertained us by playing parts from Raffles to Romeo, which was quite a span. Robinson Crusoe was another role he enjoyed, and strong men broke down and wept when he pulled a shawl over his head and recited the deathbed lines of Little Nell.

One of Mr. Day's specialties was his rendition of Poe's "The Raven" by a confused inebriate who gestured wildly as he described the bird that "still is sitting . . . sitting . . . on the pallid bust of Pallas, just above my chamber door . . . and the lamplight o'er him streaming throws his shadow on the floor."

This was as Mr. Poe intended. But then, instead of quoting the poet's concern over his own soul, that "from out that shadow . . . shall be lifted," Mr. Day manufactured a tag that at the time I was sure was the funniest ever uttered.

Pointing first to the table lamp, then to the ceiling above the door, then to his feet, showing how Mr. Poe had made a mistake in his shadows, Mr. Day said, "T'was a humpbacked, cross-eyed shadow to git cast upon the floor."

That's it. That's what Actor Day said. Hundreds held their sides. Why was it funny? Perhaps my age or the age in which I lived had something to do with my taste. But it *was* funny! So, in those simple days, was his blackface comedy, which today would have people lying, not in aisles, but in the mayor's office at City Hall. Another, proving again how easy it was to delight an audience, was "Cohen On the Telephone" in Yiddish dialect.

One night, playing at the Temple, Mr. Day had a set-to with the company manager, the details of which he seemed loathe to divulge. When I got in from school the next afternoon, my mother warned me to be quiet; poor Mr. Day was feeling ill in his room.

It was seven o'clock when my father came home and Mr. Day was still abed. Theatre curtains were raised promptly at eight those days. Father went up and spoke to Mr. Day while I watched from the hall. He spoke louder, shook our guest, got only a groan, leaned over and sniffed.

"Well!" he said. "Well, well!" He brought a pitcher of cold water from the bathroom and flung it hard at the handsome Day face. Mr. Day leaped, screaming.

The carrying power of Elias Day's voice was famous. Even in a whisper he could reach the last row in the highest gallery. But tonight as he accused my father of trying to drown him, he wasn't whispering. He could have been heard downtown in the Court House or over in Irishtown beyond the Wabash Railroad tracks. His words were unfamiliar and judging from the way my mother hurried with me downstairs, they were not fit for any ears.

"Put on your pants," my father ordered. "Your curtain goes up in forty minutes. Cab? No. You'll walk. It will do you good."

I watched them go out the gate, my father with a firm grip on the lean Day elbow, heading down Barr Street toward the theatre.

I remember a calmer summer afternoon when a famous actress named Edith Wynne Matthison and British actor Ben Greet, a lean man with dark eyes and hair, drank tea and ate small cakes with my mother and the elder Miss Margaret Hamilton beside the lilac bushes in the yard. He was talking about Shakespeare, telling the women what "The Bard," as he called him, really, *really* meant by some lines in what Mr. Greet referred to, cozily, as *The Dream.*

Mr. Greet—this was years before he became Sir Ben—and his leading lady were touring the hinterlands in an ancient morality play, *Everyman,* staged outdoors amid the mosquitoes, with the arc lights hissing and drowning out most voices. Two years later he sat again in the Hamilton Homestead yard, come this time to play the melancholy Jacques in *As You Like It,* reciting "All the world's a stage, . . .," which I had committed to memory, and he did it better than I did. Much better, I had to admit.

I was just a listener at the edges of these conversations, but an actual theatrical adventure occurred the afternoon Mr. Harry Williams, the young city editor of the *Evening Sentinel,* took me and his daughter to Swift Park. Later called Robinson, this was the town's Tivoli Garden at the turn of the century, owned by the traction company and out seven miles at the end of a streetcar line.

I was in Mr. Williams' kindly hands partly because my father no longer would go out to Swift Park, objecting to a contraption called the "Orchestrion." This oak and brass affair, with big windows all around, stood two stories high in the park's famous Pavilion, which, in turn, was an oversized gazebo overlooking the St. Joe River where it backed up behind the Feeder Canal Dam.

The monstrosity, as my father called it, played music, using the term rather loosely, being operated by a roll of punched paper like a pianola, with turning wheels and puffing bellows that forced sound out of a conglomerate array of instruments, including a harp, cornet, clarinet, violin, bass fiddle, xylophone and a battery of large and small drums. My father, who liked Wagner, the younger Strauss and Gilbert and Sullivan, fled home from this concord of sweet sounds after his first visit.

Mr. Williams and I enjoyed it, until at two o'clock he said, "Time for the theatre."

A summer vaudeville house, this "theatre" at Swift Park consisted of a roof over a stage and perhaps three or four hundred chairs, with latticed walls that admitted vagrant breezes and the always present and determined mosquitoes. A vaudeville company was playing a comedy that day which somehow involved a baby carriage; in one act it offered ten minutes of superb and radiant pratfalls. Dialogue and plot, if there were any, now escape me, but the pratfalls and what happened afterward I especially remember.

Using his press pass, Mr. Williams led us backstage, where the man who had been funniest was taking off a false nose in front of a mirror.

"You are very good, sir," Mr. Williams said. "You are a great actor. I want to see you some time in tragedy."

The man smiled and rubbed some paint off his face.

"Thank you," he said. "My name is David Warfield."

We went out to the grounds together, had a drink at the pump with the tin cup chained to it, and at the refreshment stand paused while Mr. Warfield bought all of us five-cent chocolate sodas. They were very good.

When I told my father about it that night, he added the interesting fact that a druggist friend of his down in Posey County had invented the ice-cream soda. We thought that very funny; not that anybody had invented it, but that there should be a "Posey" County. Father did not understand our amusement; Posey had been the name of a great general. It was even funnier, we thought, when we learned that the seat of Posey County was in "Hoophole Township."

I was older, much older—perhaps thirteen—when I next saw the man Harry Williams had predicted would be great. He was playing *The Music Master*. I was with my father, and we both wept when Warfield, as the old musician, was measuring out the coffee he needed to make the day begin. He was so poor he measured it twice, then frugally put some back into the tin. It caught one's throat.

This was the period when clever Hoosier playwrights such as Mr. Major and Mr. George Ade, Mr. Booth Tarkington and Mr. George Barr McCutcheon of the fabulous *Graustark* kingdom, were storming Broadway as if they were T.R.'s Rough Riders on San Juan Hill.

Naturally the people back home were proud. They were to boast to everyone, particularly visitors from out of state, that for ten years, at least, no New York theatrical season was without a hit from midwest Indiana. Sometimes it did not matter who the actors or actresses were or whether they had famous names or not. The important question was, "Which Hoosier wrote the play?"

Of Mr. Ade's many productions, the two I saw in Mr. Stouder's theatre were *The Sultan of Sulu*, laid in the Pacific Ocean, and *The County Chairman*.

Mr. Ade, who grew up in the town of Kentland, considerably west of Fort Wayne, had gone to college with the Hoosier McCutcheons, John and George, and it was cartoonist-reporter George, my mother explained, who was responsible for Mr. Ade's finding so much to laugh at instead of cry over in the Pacific Islands. Reporter McCutcheon was covering what the newspapers called the "Pacification Campaign," in the Philippines. Some readers, like our friend Mrs. Belle Taylor, protested every day that it should be called "a war against liberty"; others, agreeing with belligerent Dr. Wheelock and our young Senator Beveridge, retorted that the United States was only doing what God intended.

At any rate, several native chiefs did not want to be pacified, Mr. McCutcheon reported, giving Mr. Ade the idea for his comic opera, *The Sultan of Sulu*. For months people in our town whistled tunes from it. Men had the habit of whistling those days, instead of walking along the street glumly, worrying about taxes or whether it would rain on Saturday. Policemen on the beat, the fellow who drove Mr. Higgins' Pleasant Lake Ice Wagon, mail carriers, the man delivering Mr. Fahlsing's milk, even Uncle Gustave, a dignified bank clerk, all whistled. It was very cheerful.

The hit song in *The Sultan of Sulu* was called "R-E-M-O-R-S-E," and one line that it put into circulation, "The cold gray dawn of the morning after," Uncle Gustave said would leave its mark on the English language. *The County Chairman,* with no tunes at all and no dancing, pleased the people because it hinged on Midwest politics, a subject on which everyone rightly thought himself a specialist. Mr. Ade came to town for its opening. Like Mr. Major, he wore a pepper-and-salt suit, but unlike him, since it was summer, he sported a brightly colored band on a straw hat. He was very rich, people said.

Of all the playwrights and novelists who were bringing money back to Indiana and stashing it away in banks or buying good farm land, Mr. Ade, it seemed, wrote the fastest and hardest. He turned out books before I started to school and publishers were still bringing them out when F.D.R. reached the White House.

The first time I saw Mr. Ade's friend John McCutcheon, I thought him very handsome, and my mother said, "Yes, he has a patrician nose." Patrician or not, it sniffed out news anywhere in the world and he traveled everywhere any young fellow with itchy feet yearned to go. Not only that. When we learned where the McCutcheon brothers grew up, we envied them that piece of luck, too.

While ordinary boys, druggist's or preacher's sons like Bill Moffatt and me, went to bed in ordinary houses with no bars on the windows and doors that never had been locked, the McCutcheons had lived in a jail in Lafayette, while their father was sheriff of Tippecanoe County. They slept in the jailer's bed at night and helped handle not just drunks, but actual horse thieves, even chasing them down the street with guns. Neither Robin Hood nor that later Hoosier bold man, John Dillinger, was at large in Tippecanoe County at the time; but a jail is a jail, and Sheriff McCutcheon's in Lafayette must have been just as exciting, and the smell just as sweet, as Sheriff Grice's or Sheriff Reichelderfer's places of business were to me in Fort Wayne.

George Barr McCutcheon had enjoyed another experience as a young man that boys in my time envied. The horse-drawn traveling wagon show, barnstorming with everything from *East Lynne* to *Uncle Tom's Cabin,* was still a popular institution, in spite of its shabbiness, and it was not just foolish boys coming to no good end who ran away to join up. Even Poet James Whitcomb Riley had traveled with a medicine show; and George Barr McCutcheon, after one year in college, spent a full season splashing over Indiana roads, billed as "George M. Clifford, Comédienne." In my German community, it never was explained why the advertising signs spelled "Comédienne" in the feminine.

I was still at the tree-climbing age when I first saw Mr. Ade and Mr. George Barr McCutcheon. They were with Senator Beveridge, whom anybody at any age would recognize because he made so many speeches. I was probably twelve years old and for no particular reason had shinnied up to the top of a buckeye tree across the alley behind Mr. Frank Deck's Sample Room. This clean, wholesome establishment was around the corner from the old car barns on Chestnut Street and only a block from our front gate.

My position in the tree gave me a splendid view of the Sample Room's back yard, which had a grape arbor, a high board fence overgrown with trumpet vines, two flat-topped "stink" trees—the common man's name for what highbrow gardeners called "ailanthus"—and several iron tables with benches. Mr. Deck's place was popular with everyone except ladies. Why so many men chose it for discussions I did not know, for Mr. Deck never became involved in any strife himself, particularly when it was going on across the bar from him. He always meticulously obeyed the laws and never was raided for infractions of the criminal code. He did not encourage lady customers; in fact he was known to inform them that he could get along nicely, thank you, without their patronage. He was not being personal. He just didn't like Miss Carrie Nation, the direct-action Prohibitionist from Kansas.

This afternoon in this idyllic setting, Playwrights McCutcheon and Ade, Governor Winfield Durbin, Senator Beveridge —his admirers always said "golden-tongued Senator Beveridge" —sat around a table covered with fresh white linen instead of its usual oilcloth. They were drinking whatever was the popular beverage of the moment, probably either Berghoff's or Centlivre's beer, and discussing politics, not the theatre or literature. The conversation was over my head, but the longer I listened the more I became convinced that in part, at least, they didn't understand themselves. Senator Beveridge, it seemed to me then, was always running for re-election, and besides, I was more interested in Dramatist Ade.

Close on the heels of Mr. Ade's two productions, Booth Tarkington's first play, *Monsieur Beaucaire,* came to town— "another great drama by another great Hoosier," the *News* said. One of the local clubs sponsored it and Mr. Tarkington himself rode the Lake Erie and Western up from Indianapolis to join in the ladies' celebration. He never spoke in public if he could help it, my mother explained, but this day he stepped out on the Temple stage and bowed. This was the first time I ever had seen duelling blades in action, on the stage or anywhere else. So more than his bows or the elaborate scenery or the jovial characters throwing dice, the sight of the young Frenchman with blood staining his white coat, parrying the thrusts of a wicked cavalier, I thought was worth the money.

When I went to see *Alice of Old Vincennes,* my mother was with me, and with her historical bent, she was disappointed in

it. She thought that Mr. Maurice Thompson, its author, had
dressed up Indiana's drab frontier with too much glamour.
The surrender of the old French fort and Vincennes trading
post to General George Rogers Clark, she said, had no charming overtones in her history books and Mr. Thompson, she
thought, dealt too much with sentiment.

However that might be, Mr. Thompson was different from
the other Civil War heroes among us. For a shocking reason.
He had worn the Gray instead of the Blue; and in spite of
that, he had dared come back to Indiana. He had lived the
disgrace down, Grandfather Goshorn said. So completely that,
when he died, he was the only Confederate soldier whose
funeral an Indiana G.A.R. post ever attended in a body. And
that, Grandfather remarked, proved something or other. For
my part, I thought it would have made a nice scene for a
play.

Our newspapers, Sunday or daily, had no comic strips as
such, but they did have series of characters making wise or
pointed or funny remarks. Among them were Playwright Ade's
"Fables in Slang," Kin Hubbard's hayseed farmer "Abe
Martin" teetering on a barbed wire fence in Brown County,
and Finley Peter Dunne's saloon keeper, "Mr. Dooley," whom
my mother liked to quote.

People of all ages, living in the Homesteads or in Nebraska
across the river, put down their pennies for a paper if for
nothing else than to see what these characters were up to; and
conversations on the street often began with the question,
"Did you read 'Mr. Dooley' today or 'Abe Martin'?"

I liked Mr. Ade's plays better than anything else he wrote,
but he did introduce a number of beautiful new slang words
to my age group. He could talk in print like a Lutheran
preacher or a Pennsy section hand, and he used capital letters
where school teachers claimed no capitals belonged, like "A
Good Folly is Worth What You Pay for It," or "Early to Bed
and Early to Rise and You will Meet very few Interesting
People."

Also, in Mr. Ade's "Fables," unlike Mr. Aesop's, virtue did
not always win. If his miserable character, Sister Mae,

scrubbed floors and stayed pure, while her beautiful but dumb
sister had fun, it was the sister who married rich and hired
poor Mae to work in her kitchen. Just like life, I overheard
Uncle Gustave tell Mother.

The sentences by Kin Hubbard in the Indianapolis paper to
which my father subscribed—the "Kin" was not short for
President McKinley as some of the President's admirers at
mother's teas thought, but from Hubbard's middle name,
McKinney—used pen-and-ink drawings as well as words. The
drawings made one laugh and the words packed a wallop, so
plain no one needed to explain what they meant.

They were a family affair, with something for everyone to
quote. For my banker uncle, it was young Tell Binkley, who
skipped with the Trust Company's funds just because he was
so popular he had to invest heavily in car repairs. Which
served him right, too, if he was so high-toned he couldn't hitch
up a horse any longer.

If you were Grandfather Goshorn and had no patience with
politicians, you quoted Tipton Bud, "who's got only one more
lodge to join 'fore he runs fer county clerk." As for the crazy
new X-ray machines, which everyone was arguing about,
Abe's comment on the poor devil who fell off the hay wagon
was that he died before the doctor could X-ray his teeth.
Readers laughed, too, at Tilford Moots, who "sez his wife's
mother is comin' t' visit them anyhow." In our house, where
there were no grandmothers, only grandfathers, this remark
had to be explained.

Naturally the people in town did not leave all writing and
acting to experts. They never had done so. The town throbbed
with drama. Husbands and wives together, at Library Hall in
Cathedral Square and Temple Theatre, had staged *Pinafore*,
Trial by Jury, Iolanthe and other works as fast as a pair of
newcomers named Gilbert and Sullivan wrote them. My father
boasted that he had participated in *Trial by Jury* nine months
after its London debut.

The drama my mother planned about her hero, Anthony
Wayne, never got past the first act, four children having
spoiled her schedule, but her friend Mrs. Tom Creighton did

write and direct *Reckless Ralph of Rattlesnake Run,* which
was cheered at home but never got a toehold on Broadway.

Drama circles and Shakespeare reading clubs often pro-
duced home-brewed plays, some of them so topical, so full of
local innuendo, that drama in court followed drama on the
stage.

"Like the one in Aboite Township, two or three years after
you were born," Grandfather Goshorn recollected. "A woman
named Crawford slandered a gentleman in a rival club. At
least he swore she did. She read a line that said, 'There sits
Christian Ambler with a reigning new moon for a nose.' It
enraged him.

"So the next week Mr. Ambler replied. Wrote a play himself
and said something about Miss Crawford having a half-ounce
of brains and never combed her hair. Both sued. Squire Harry
France heard the case. A regular Hoosier Solomon.

"Both had been wrong, he decided. Each should pay the
other ten dollars. And if this playwriting foolishness continued, he would stop all plays."

"Did he?" I asked.

"Wasn't necessary," Grandfather said. "Not in Aboite Township, anyway. The next week somebody put on a play where
the hero screamed 'Zounds!' at the end of each line. It stopped
the show."

14

EASELS, BOOKS, A
BURGLAR AND
MR. RILEY

✱↣✤↣✱↣✤↣✱↣✤↣✱↣✤↣✱↣✤↣✱↣✤↣✱↣✤↣✱↣✤↣✱↣✤↣✱↣✤

THREE WOMEN owned the Lehman Book Store. One was Miss Jennie Lehman, who hailed from Mrs. Gene Stratton Porter's Limberlost region, down the G. R. and I. Railroad. The second was Miss Alice Habecker, two-hundred-and-fifty-pound principal of the Hanna Grade School, a remarkable individual whose excess poundage made it difficult for her to walk, but who pumped her bicycle nearly two miles each day to school. My mother, who did not appear on the book store letterhead, was the third owner.

A newspaper and magazine dealer on Calhoun Street had offered his rundown stand for sale. His asking price, about seven hundred and fifty dollars, was high, but the three women scraped it together. They scrubbed out the place, scattered new rag rugs on the floor, threw out the trash among the magazines and substituted *Atlantic, Harper's, Littell's Living Age, Century, Scribner, The Bookman* and *The North American Review.*

Miss Lehman, a pretty, dark-eyed young woman who had come up from the Swiss settlement of Berne to sell ribbons, yard goods and linens in Mr. DeWald's Dry Goods Store, ten hours a day, for six days and seven dollars a week, knew how to cut costs and sell merchandise, but she was not especially interested in books as books. To her went the job as general manager.

Miss Habecker served as bookkeeper, my ex-librarian mother as book buyer and later as buyer of the prints—etchings, engravings, mezzotints, fine lithographs and aquatints.

A boy, watching and listening in the back room when a Chicago salesman was offering fine specimens and a woman as discriminating as my mother was bargaining for the best prices, learned quickly to distinguish between a steel engraving and a copperplate, an unwiped etching and a state-of-plate, a drypoint and a stipple. Particularly if there were an etching press at home and all his life he had heard excited talk of prints.

An etching press stood in the middle of the room behind the library in the last house we lived in during my boyhood, its rollers squeezing a flat, steel bed. An iron wheel, big as a riverboat steering wheel, had spokes on which we hung, contributing gravity power.

"Etching is a catty art," Mother used to say. "You scratch the wax and bite the plate, a completely feline process."

Artists good and bad used our room, sketching on waxed copper plates, "biting" them in the tank of diluted nitric acid, and after the acid ate out the scratches, scraping off the wax, rubbing in ink and printing their results on our press.

Saturday was press day. My father, who did not pretend to be an artist, but who by nature lacked patience for anyone who did not wipe clean the surface of a plate, handled the paper, kept damp all week between moist blotters. We children helped. One Christmas, receiving three neatly waxed plates, I went to work fast. But I caught the amusement in one artist's eye when she saw my finished work, and I never tried again.

Even before the purchase of the book store, Mother and various friends had bought prints. From second-hand bins all over town, for nickels and dimes, they had collected masterpieces—and many of them proved to be—hung them on their walls, traded, entertained at "print parties."

It had been a red-letter day when they discovered the ten-cent bin in Mr. Siemon's store. They had argued with him that his price was much too low but in accent thick as *Schmierkase*, he had demanded, "Who Ever Hears of a Whistler? *Ja*, it is ten cents, or leave it."

Not only did his disdain for prints appall the women; so did his ignorance of local history. Evidently no one had ever told him that an ancestor of James McNeil Whistler had been commander at the old Anthony Wayne Fort.

Within a few months, the new owners of the store had branched out from magazines to three or four shelves of books—the classics chiefly at first. Classics would always sell, canny Miss Lehman figured. After the classics they put in other books: poems bound in limp red Moroccan leather by the respectable Hoosier sisters, Phoebe and Alice Cary; Mark Twain's *Joan of Arc;* and for youthful buyers books like *Black Beauty*, the story of a horse. The women were pleased but not surprised that patronage grew. The town had enough intelligent citizens to make a really good book store pay, my mother insisted. It took perseverance and years, but eventually it became and was for several decades the largest book store in the state north of Indianapolis.

Soon after the first books came a *Quarterly Review*, a daring literary innovation for a town that not too many years earlier had possessed only a "ladies' reading room." Most of its articles appeared under my mother's initials, L. G. D., and people learned to trust them. She would not say that a book was worth reading unless she had read all its pages herself and considered it so. It did no good for Miss Lehman to urge a "nice review" on a novel that the book buyer called junk; and if Mother ordered any copies of it, they would be only a few, as she said, "for backstairs reading."

Local merchants never had been shy in boosting what the enthusiastic Commercial Club called "our magnificent mercantile establishments . . . everything available, from a hickory shirt to a case of the finest Maryland whiskey." People with money in their pockets came from all over the state to buy imported French wallpaper from L. O. Hull, a new set of brass-fitted carriage harness from Senator Robert Bell, jewelry from

August Bruder, "as fine as Tiffany's." The advertisements that
began to appear in the back of the *Quarterly* were published
admittedly for profit, not for literary merit. No one intended
them to be amusing.

The Sydney C. Lumbard Agency was a faithful contributor
to the *Quarterly,* probably because Mrs. Lumbard, widow of
the founder, was my mother's friend. Mr. Lumbard had been
a man of parts. He played on the first baseball team, ran with
the hand-drawn hose reel in the first fire department and
helped organize the elegant Wayne Club, which had a big
auditorium on the third floor up a narrow stairway—only God
by watching over it prevented fires.

Mr. Lumbard put in the first telephone exchange, with
twenty instruments, and opened it formally with his wife
singing solos to the subscribers. My father always said that no
man in town had a higher sense of morality, for when he
helped poor people by lending them money, Mr. Lumbard
charged low interest rates and never made things difficult for
the down and out. Of course, the widow of a gentleman such
as he would help the new book store.

Mr. Bruder, our leading jeweler, who was known as a
"confirmed bachelor," until then had rarely advertised in anything. For years he ran an exclusive shop and lived an
exclusive life in a furnished room. Like Mr. Tiffany, he never
advertised in the daily press. Why should he? The carriage
trade knew that 18-karat gold in his store really was 18-karat.
But surprisingly he did put a business card in the *Quarterly,*
with great style and dignity to be sure; simply his name, the
word "Jeweler," and the address of his shop at Calhoun and
Wayne Streets.

The advertisement that stirred one's fancy, and perhaps
nightmares, was that of Mr. Hull.

This pioneer merchant handled paints and window blinds as
well as wallpaper and was expert in fixing up the parlor walls
with "French appliqué." The high point of his advertisement
in the *Quarterly* was not the offer of "Finest Work, Prompt
Service and Lowest Prices," but the Hull trademark.

In those unhurried days, merchants often stood carved

figures on the narrow sidewalks in front of their business places, and nobody wrote to the mayor to complain. People simply walked around them. Mr. Hull's famous figure, six feet tall, chunky around the waistline, elegant in frock coat and striped pants, with silk top hat in one hand, walking stick in the other and a large shirt stud beneath his string tie, was carved of wood and neatly painted.

But instead of a head, out of the gates-ajar collar came a huge hand some two feet long, with an oversized index finger pointing off into the distance, presumably at someone needing L. O. Hull's wallpaper. When I think of the cold chills it gave an innocent boy, I can only pity the gentlemen who had remained too long at the saloon around the corner, then met face to face the accusing finger. Reproduced in the *Quarterly*, it looked magnificent. Did it sell wallpaper? Who knows? At least it brought advertising revenue to the struggling book store magazine.

Merchants' signs were of all kinds. Perhaps the most famous was a big wooden dog standing on a wooden base outside Ward's China and Crockery Store on Columbia Street. It was a pleasant enough beast, and the store's slogan was painted at its feet: "I'm Ward's Dog. Whose Dog Are You?"

Wooden watches two feet in diamater hung in front of jewelers' shops, with the hands painted permanently at twenty minutes past eight, which supposedly was the hour when Lincoln died. Butcher shops showed pleasant-looking cows, their buttocks enlarged to suggest juicy steaks—undoubtedly it was merely an accident that the sign-painting artists gave them such soulful expressions, as if pleading with passersby please to become vegetarians.

One oculist's sign was a six-foot pair of wooden glasses, neatly gilded, with a pair of eyes widely staring out of the frames. The eyes were light blue and seemed once to have belonged to a giant fish, long dead. Dentists used sets of grinning teeth in a yard-long arc, and the wooden horses of the harness-makers were guaranteed to impede traffic; one on Columbia Street was accoutered in genuine leather. Mr. M. App's shoe store was marked by a wooden boot, kept painted

a shiny black and three feet tall; and wooden Indians guarded
the doors of all tobacco shops except Mr. John Carl's. Instead
of an Indian, Mr. Carl had a five-foot, carved, brightly painted
Punch, hook-nosed, hunchbacked grinning ear to big ear and
holding out an inviting handful of wooden cigars.

The Lehman Book Store could afford no such gaudy or
wealthy monument. The Hull reproduction in the *Quarterly*
had to do.

Miss Lehman put money in the bank through hard work,
her own, and that of everyone around her, including me,
whose job it became five nights after school and all day
Saturday, to convert myself into a delivery truck. I earned
every penny of my seventy-five cents a week. For I had to run,
not walk, from school, to pick up bundles, packages, magazines
and newspapers. They were to be distributed on a long route
and I never left the store, staggering under my load, that Miss
Lehman did not tell me to be sure and hurry.

Dr. Mommer, a dentist with a second-floor office on Calhoun Street, took the Chicago *Inter-Ocean*. His stop usually
was my first, up a long wooden stairway, and invariably he
thundered at me for being late. He may have been having fun
with me but it never seemed so. Mrs. J. R. Meriwether, a
grande dame in the D.A.R. who lived in the last big house on
West Washington, took a New York newspaper and all the
women's magazines, which were heavy. It was always dark
when I rang her doorbell—you never tossed the bundle onto
her porch more than once—and it was a good mile back to the
store. I was cold and hungry and often my feet were wet.
There were trolleys, to be sure, but the conductors enforced a
ridiculous rule about boys not hanging onto the side. The book
store was frugal with nickels for carfare, and Miss Lehman
closed promptly at six o'clock so that her saleswoman, Miss
Bertha Griebel, could get home in time to cook supper.

I had to deliver one magazine each week to a rich-looking
fat man whose first name was Pete and who lived in the West
Side halfway to Mrs. Meriwether's. He always greeted me
pleasantly and once offered me a glass of beer, which he
seemed to think was a great joke.

Pete was a smart operator, Uncle Gustave explained later, a professional gambler who did not content himself with going out to the Driving Park in summer to bet on the horses. He made a good living all year round at home, playing poker and shooting dice on a green-topped table in an upstairs room at the rear of his own house.

One night when it was raining, Pete wasn't at home so I took the magazine back to the book store where my mother, waiting to walk home with me, saw the lurid cover.

"Where on earth did you get that?" she demanded, snatching it from me. I told her I was delivering it to Pete.

"Jennie Lehman!" my mother said in her sternest voice. "Did you ask my son to deliver that filthy trash to a professional gambler?" And to me: "Don't you ever go near that house again!"

So poor Bill Stellhorn, forty-five years old and tired, who worked full-time at the store, had to take over the job.

There was a great deal of gambling in Fort Wayne and Mother's talk about it was not new. She considered it one of the original sins, not that she objected to card-playing, but she believed that professionals used marked cards and loaded dice and took advantage of working men.

Grandfather Goshorn had aroused her fury one day when I was too young to go alone to a barber shop, and he took me. The shop was on Jefferson Street near the corner of Calhoun. An open door led to a saloon at the rear, and another open door from it to a game room, where a pleasant man with a bad cough spun for my amusement what I later learned was a roulette wheel.

My mother liked the haircut, but when I told her where I got it, she demanded of Grandfather, "Why did you take him there?"

"Because it's the best barber shop," he answered.

She had no need to worry about poker. She knew that I had not been smart enough to learn to play it when Grandfather Goshorn tried to teach me. Poker was one of his delights. He liked to meet his cronies in the back room of "Schwäbenfritz's place" on East Berry Street. Poker, Grandfather said, was relaxing, but expensive if one had not grasped its fine points early in life.

So when I was about seven, he set out to acquaint me with the game. After several weeks I heard him tell my mother that perhaps I was "a little young" to grasp it. But anyone, he said, could quickly learn casino so he would start me on it.

"Even women play it," he explained.

But casino also proved too difficult or dull, and Grandfather picked up the cards one evening, looked at me steadily and cleared his throat.

"Some people," he said, "otherwise normal mentally, just have no knack for cards. You are one of these. So never in any circumstances let yourself be hornswoggled into playing any card game. Poker in particular. It would prove too costly."

Bill Stellhorn, who had to take over the shame of delivering Gambler Pete's magazine, was a meek little man with his thin hair slicked down who wore red suspenders, swept the floors before the store opened at eight o'clock each morning, framed pictures, stoked the furnace, washed the windows, unpacked books, strove nobly but with no success to keep the plumbing operating. He had enough to do without becoming a delivery boy, he and old Miss Lehman and a good job was waiting at the oil tank works. So she canceled the gambler's subscription; there wasn't enough profit in that long walk anyhow.

Miss Lehman abhorred idleness with the same vigor my mother opposed professional gambling. Even an author, sitting uneasily at a table near the front door to autograph a new masterpiece, seemed to annoy Miss Lehman, who had definite ideas on the value not only of hours but of minutes. But her approach was subtle.

Once Gene Stratton Porter, her *Song of the Cardinal* hitting a sales peak, was rubbing writer's cramp out of her right hand when Miss Lehman spotted her.

"While you're sitting there doing nothing," she told the startled author, "why don't you come over here and begin dusting these shelves?"

Meekly, Mrs. Porter obeyed.

By that time this ambitious woman had moved down from the flat above her husband's drug store in Geneva and was mining tons of pure literary gold out of nearby Limberlost swamp. My father, who was traveling for a wholesale drug company, used to stop alternate weeks and chat with Charley Porter.

"Charley can't understand that wife of his," he would say when he got home. "He gave her a Kodak and she began to take pictures of birds and it's turned her into a writer." At the top of her million-dollar career, with her stack of happy endings miles high above the swamp, she remained, so far as my father was concerned, "Charley Porter's wife."

My mother never had read any of Mrs. Porter's books, which made her out of step with the marketing world, if not the literary. It did not mar their friendship, however, and one summer day the two were sitting in the shade on the north side of our house on Barr and Lewis Streets. A double row of tall elms kept the morning sun off that yard, and my mother had an iron table and a few chairs there, where she often served iced tea to all ages.

"What's the name of your new book, Gene?" my mother asked.

"*Freckles*," said Mrs. Porter.

"Oh, yes. I tried to read it."

"Don't try," said Druggist Charley Porter's wife. "You just couldn't like it, Laura. I didn't write it for you."

"How many copies have you sold?"

"Half a million, so far," Mrs. Porter replied. "I sometimes think they must use them for paving blocks."

Artists found a good market in the Lehman Book Store. There was a sizeable company of them in Indiana, practicing various banches of the graphic arts: painters in oil and watercolor, etchers and engravers, those who occasionally polished a slab of marble to prepare a lithograph, or drew delicate illustrations in India ink for a new volume for busy Indianapolis publisher Bobbs.

These men and women and their writing friends often gathered on the hills of Brown County, where forests and plumbing were primeval. Brown was the only Indiana county without a railroad, and its few narrow highways, running straight up and down, were either deep mud or strewn with boulders. Near the hill towns of Gnaw Bone, Bean Blossom, Stone Head and Younk, where characters to paint or write about abounded, interlopers with easels, paint and typewriters built small cabins.

With transportation just beginning to advance from the mule age to horses, no visitors got in anyone's way. The hills made dramatic sawtooth horizons, and spring and fall the artists broke out pastels or oils, with an extra tube of crimson madder in season.

Coming into the Book Store occasionally was landscape painter Otto Stark, a wispy man with wispy whiskers and a wispy voice, who looked at his palette through thick glasses worn far down on his nose, and who could outwalk a husky ten-year-old every morning of the week.

Also at the store and in and out of our living room, I saw J. Otis Adams and his pleasant artist wife, Winifred, whose sons were my occasional playmates. Mr. and Mrs. Adams cheerfully avoided the Brown County rush and spent golden autumns at their country house at Brookville. Mr. Adams, a lean man, walked with a limp; gored by a bull when a boy, he had never fully recovered. One shoe was built up, and he braced himself with a cane, but he did not let what he considered a trifling infirmity keep him from carrying his easel and box of paints.

Mr. Adams liked to paint nature at its rawest; apple blossoms and contented cows were not his meat. He preferred bare branches of old oak trees writhing in wind, or the break-up of winter with an ice gorge choking an Indiana stream. Mrs. Adams painted, too. She liked to do close-up portraits of May-apple blossoms and Indian pipes in moist spring woods. She had skill with watercolors, giving them the depth and rich tones usually associated only with oils.

Other Hoosier artists I met and admired and tried to imitate were Homer Gordon Davisson and Theodore C. Steele—"Ted" to his fellows. Mr. Steele was born on Bean Blossom Creek at Spencer, just thirty miles downstream from Brown County, but in spite of being at home in that locale, he painted more portraits than landscapes. Mr. Davisson came into the store frequently. A long lock of hair was always falling between his eyes and his glasses as he talked to the women, and he would as soon have crawled on his hands and knees around Monument Circle in Indianapolis as be without his paints in Brown County when October made the forests blush.

None of these men ever hurried, ever became impatient or annoyed at the way a picture was framed at the Lehman Book Store, or by the price agreed for its sale. I remember no poet or novelist taking time out to tell a boy how or how not to write poetry or novels. But most of the artists were quick to pick up a pencil or charcoal stick and guide a grubby left hand over paper. Conversations were of simple things. Such minor disagreements as turned up concerned beauty and its meaning and were conducted dispassionately without table pounding. Volcanic subjects like "manifest destiny" they left to more vociferous souls.

Closer than the Steeles and Davissons, Starks and Adamses, were our neighbors in the houses across the street or across the block, the women artists in the talented Hamilton family. In one generation there were seven remarkable Hamilton sisters and female cousins. Miss Jessie and Miss Agnes, in their long, narrow studio up three flights of stairs in their tall house, did portraits and still lifes by the uncertain heat of a wood stove— Jessie in oils, Agnes in watercolor. We all sat for them, for the most part patiently. We were both flattered and interested, and for ten years, at least, it was a rare occasion not to see an unfinished portrait of a child in our family on Miss Jessie's easel.

Their sister Miss Katherine, my mother's particular friend, never painted, but in addition to translating French and German poetry into English verse, she collected fine prints and rare books. With my mother she prowled shops and second-hand stores hunting treasures, somewhat as Historian Jake Dunn and I prowled the slippery banks of Leo Creek.

Their cousin Miss Nora, a soft-spoken woman in a paint-spattered smock, lived for any and every form of art: pen or

pencil, watercolors or oils or etching needle. Her portrait of me
at the age of five still hangs on my living-room wall. It was
Artist Nora and her sister Dr. Alice who at Christmas and
New Year's joyfully shepherded the twins and me to early and
late church services.

New Year's Eve, for the music and spectacle, we visited
Immaculate Conception Cathedral at midnight. Christmas
morning at six o'clock we admired the decorations in St. Paul's
Lutheran, later to be the scene of Grandfather Adam's elaborate funeral. Not only were there great fir trees on each side of
the chancel, but they recklessly held hundreds of lighted wax
candles. Certainly Someone Upstairs heard the children's choir
singing "Bless Us and Preserve Us," for when St. Paul's finally
did burn, it was not at Christmas time, no one was in the
building, and candles had nothing to do with it.

We were living then only a hundred yards from its door.
The roof fell in at dawn but no one in our family wakened.
That I missed this gaudy blaze was one of the great dis-
appointments of my youth.

Even as children we stood a little in awe of Dr. Alice
Hamilton, a handsome young woman in a crisp white shirtwaist, with large dark eyes and an unquenchable curiosity.
She was the first woman on the Harvard medical faculty, the
genius who discovered which flies carried what disease, that
filth was part of most food processing and that careless use of
paint in industry could cause lead poisoning.

For parts of the year, Dr. Alice would be in Germany or
Austria, then home for three or four months to work on her
notes. Her battles against starvation in the needle trades,
against child labor, infant mortality and the twelve-hour
sweatshop day did not surprise the friends who lived close to
her.

Dr. Alice's two sisters, Miss Edith and Miss Madge, each
unusual later in her own field, were as willing as she to enter-
tain neighborhood children. It was Miss Edith, the future
Citizen of Athens, when I was eight years old on Mackinac
Island, where we were spending the summer before the arrival

of brother Gus, who first taught me to say "Mack-i-naw," never "Mack-i-nack," as uninitiated do to this day.

The Spanish-American War had just ended, and sitting on the porch steps, she helped me patiently day after day with my patriotic coloring book. We did not agree on all points. She thought that I should color Admiral Dewey's uniform blue, not orange and purple as I planned. Too little of Admiral Sampson's uniform showed around his ostentatious whiskers, and Admiral Schley had a hangdog look and hardly any whiskers at all.

Miss Edith was a reasonable woman, but she did spoil some of my more charming color schemes. All the navy wore blue, she insisted, but what I did to Santiago's hero, General William Rufus Shafter, hardly mattered. I gave him the full treatment, including three shades of red, and Miss Edith allowed her friendliness to overwhelm the truth and called it beautiful.

I was older, just ten, when Miss Madge, always an educator, allowed me to badger her into reading over and over from a book in her library a frightful juvenile verse about boys of various ages.

"What to do with a boy of two . . . of three . . . of six . . ." and so on, until finally: "What to do with boys of ten? They are no longer boys, but MEN!" It fed my ego and I helped her bear down hard on the last word.

Sketches and etchings by Hamilton women—their books were to come later—sold well in the Lehman Store.

If you hung around the store long enough with eyes and ears open, you learned facts of life as well as of art and literature. Customers liked to talk about writers. Not only about their books, but which of them planned a divorce, which one was hounded by bill collectors, who was fishing for channel cats with General Lew Wallace in his houseboat down on the Tippecanoe, or having the bourbon boiled out of him at Martinsville Sanitarium, who was in town for the day standing on the corner talking—even how Mrs. Porter hated her real name, Geneva, and changed it to Gene when she came of age.

Occasionally there even was excitement in the store itself. Profits were too thin for the owners to take thievery lightly, not just pilfering of books from the tables or shelves but tapping the cash drawer for a day's receipts. Burglaries continued for several weeks before an indignant Miss Lehman quietly went to see the police.

Detective Pete Cooling responded. He would spend nights in the building until the villain, who must have found a key, was caught. It did not occur to Detective Cooling to conceal himself in the store itself. Evidently he had been reading books. For he suggested, in a whisper, that he could cut a hole in the floor of a vacant room above, and from that vantage point peep down and discover the culprit.

Dissuaded from this by Miss Lehman, who saw enough tragic loss in the pilfering from the cash drawer without having to repair an ornamental pressed-sheet-iron ceiling, too, Detective Cooling took up a strategic position behind a stack of empty book crates.

Three nights he waited, and then the *Evening News* reported: "Detective Pete Cooling, who was hiding in the Lehman Book Store on Calhoun Street to catch a thief, was awakened at 5:30 this morning by the stealthy entrance of a man. The officer leaped on him just as he finished rifling the cash drawer, and when the young fellow showed fight, knocked him out with a well-aimed right to the chin."

The loot that day was $1.45.

It was at the book store that I learned how much money Mr. James Whitcomb Riley's first book had made: $166. This was an eye opener to me. It indicated that writing could be as lucrative a profession as preaching and getting free passes on the railroads. The book had been *The Old Swimmin' Hole,* published long before I was around to read verse or anything else, but it still was selling.

"A hundred copies last Christmas," Miss Lehman reported.

Mother had brought Mr. Edward Eggleston's *The Hoosier Schoolmaster* home from the store and dropped it in front of me, carelessly, as if pretending she really didn't care whether I looked at it or not. I did read it. But I didn't think people would talk the odd way they did for Mr. Eggleston.

I enjoyed Riley. He spoke what he called "plain hoss sense" about hop toads, corn fields, back country roads, loafers at the railroad station, fresh butter in a churn for fresh bread and the flags hanging limp on a hot summer day at the circus parade. I liked his word, "folks." It fitted the people in our town who lay in hammocks between two apple trees in the back yard or sat in rocking chairs on the front porch of a summer evening, if the mosquitoes weren't too bad.

Mr. Riley was the first author I ever met. He was the "Children's Poet," and was to speak at an afternoon meeting at the Princess Rink, an arena at Main and Griffith Streets for ice skaters in winter and roller skaters in summer, and the largest auditorium in town for all seasons.

I was four or five years old and Mrs. Rupert was in charge of me. She was a plump, chuckling woman, free and easy at handing out cookies, who today would be called a baby sitter. Her husband, Bill, was a mechanic at Louis Rastetter's woodworking plant, and they lived in a small, unpretentious house with square insets of intriguing colored glass along the top of the parlor window, looking out on DeWald Street. This was near the home of Charley Nestle, alias Commodore Foote, and his sister, Eliza. On ordinary days when I was in Mrs. Rupert's care, and the "Children's Poet" was not speaking, she would walk me slowly past the Nestle house so that I could admire the Commodore and the Faerie Queen sitting like oversized dolls in their undersized chairs in the well-raked yard.

The afternoon of the Riley lecture, my mother had supplied Mrs. Rupert with two tickets. It was a hot day and a long walk to the rink. We had seats in the front row, so close to the low platform that I could touch it. The poet was introduced by Mr. Justin Study, which was the appropriate name of the new superintendent of schools. Speakers liked to be introduced by Mr. Study, Uncle Gustave said, because his voice was rather small, to match his manner, so that anyone with an ordinary voice who followed him sounded like Cicero.

The introduction was long. When Mr. Study finally ended,

Mr. Riley walked to the front of the stage, just above me, and read from a book in his left hand while he gestured with his right. Then he dragged forward a walnut rocker and prepared to sit down. But before he did so, he leaned over, patted me on the head, picked me up, and to my astonishment and Mrs. Rupert's, put me on his lap.

Pretending to talk only to me, he launched into:

"Little Orphant Annie come to our house to stay,
To wash the cups and saucers up and brush the crumbs away."

He was a stocky man with a big voice; he wore a gold watch chain across the front of his clean white vest, and a broad black cord fell from his rimless glasses, perched on a long, red nose. His knees were knobby and hard to sit on, and he held me tight, probably to keep me from escaping. He smelled deliciously of something which long afterward I identified as a combination of good Kentucky bourbon and well-chewed cloves.

His eyes looked pink to me, and I thought I saw in them proof of his love of children. I couldn't have been more wrong. He detested children, but it was years before I knew that astonishing fact. He wrote about children, but his interest in them was strictly commercial.

I saw Mr. Riley once later on the street. He wore a long, dark overcoat with deep pockets; and when he paused on the corner to talk to my parents, he lifted one elbow, indicated a pocket, and ordered, "Dig." I obeyed. So did all the other "nasty little brats," as he called us in off-record conversations with his good friend Dr. McCoullough. The peanuts we found were unshelled and there was always fresh popcorn.

Our newspapers, particularly the *Sentinel,* which had a kind heart and could turn down no one with an offering, printed reams of what my mother called mostly bad verse. Perhaps because Fort Wayne was a railroad town, much of the "poetry" concerned wrecks, which my age group found so exciting that whether it scanned or rhymed did not matter. One frantic effort, by a farmer down in Kingsland, limped through fifty bloody stanzas about a ghastly collision between

two interurban trains. Another, by a switchman on the
Wabash Railroad, celebrated the head-on crash of two crack
Pennsylvania "flyers" on the St. Mary's River Bridge. But the
one that Hoosiers with any state pride called "the worst poem
in any language," was "The Monon Wreck."

This was written by a loquacious farmer-schoolteacher
whom a nearby editor, with tongue in cheek, had dubbed
"The Bard of Alamo."

Until forbidden, we ran around the house chanting:

> *"And yonder in the wreck I see*
> *A man that's pinioned by the knee,*
> *And hear him calmly for to say,*
> *'Cut, oh, cut, my leg away.'"*

And then, more loudly:

> *"Quite as cold as a frozen chunk*
> *A lady's heart upon a stump."*

Such sweet poesy called for gestures and we supplied them
generously. Grade school "elocution" teachers, like Aunt Dolly
who married Uncle Gustave, had taught us the appropriate
motions for any situation. If you were angry, you clenched
your fist; ashamed, you hung your head; exalted, you clasped
your hands and looked skyward.

We used the "exalted" gesture for the poem by Mr. John
Hay called "Little Breeches." This gifted statesman, born
down at Salem near the Ohio River, was to be remembered by
the nation for "opening the door" to China. Such a triumph
might be important to other people, including the Chinese, but
to us in Mr. Hay's poetic words: "Saving a little child and
fotching him to his own, is a durn sight better business than
loafing around the Throne."

Or opening any doors anywhere. It was a fine poem, we
thought, and Mr. Hay's five-year-old "Little Breeches" was an
extraordinarily fine fellow.

"Little Breeches," rescued from death, asked for so little.
When his brave saviours found him huddled among his sheep
in a blizzard, he did not demand hot food, dry pants or a warm

bed. He wanted "only a chaw of terbaccy, an' that's what's the matter with me."

Mr. Hays' character "Jim Bludsoe" we venerated almost as highly. The Bard of Alamo might glorify train wrecks, but Mr. Hay's steamboat fire was just as real and even more exciting. His "Jim Bludsoe" was a "keerless man" in his talk. He never "flunked" and he never lied. And when he told his mates he would hold the ship's "nozzle agin the bank till the last galoot's ashore," his mates "knowed he would keep his word." He did, and burned to death himself.

"And Christ," Mr. Hay concluded, "ain't a-goin' to be too hard on a man that died for men."

Having a parent who owned a piece of a book store and invited interesting guests to tea was a blessing we probably failed to realize at the moment. The book store parent might think that reading the Bard of Alamo was a shameful waste of time. But she never snatched a book out of anyone's hands, saying, "You can't read that! It shouldn't be on any shelf!"

Our favorite characters could wear shining armor, Shawnee war paint or country sunbonnets, dwell in French castles or in the Limberlost—so far as we were concerned it didn't matter where they lived or what they wore. Just so they walked and breathed. Or so far as our mother was concerned, just so we read.

The villains were blackhearted, but no one ever confused them with the heroes. Scoundrels always ended in jail, thugs were thugs, and they were caught red-handed on the last page. You could be sure of that. We lived on speaking terms with greatness and with the humble and unwashed. Art, literature, poetry and the police paddy wagon were part of our exciting lives. We confused them, confused yesterday, today and tomorrow, confused events, men's lives, their names and purposes, for we were very young.

My sister Dorothy rushed in to my mother one afternoon when a print buyer from the Chicago Art Institute arrived.

"Mother!" she panted. "Mr. Albrecht Dürer is at the door!"

15

ABOUT IT
AND ABOUT . . .

I T WAS the Age of Argument in our town and all over America, with an argumentative people fumbling with new experiences and untried ideas. This was a louder era than any Age of Reason, long ago and far away. Hoosier hills echoed dialectics and discussions, disputation and debate. No questions went unanswered, even if no two answers were alike, and nearly everyone had a wonderful solution for practically everything.

Arguments bit off, chewed up and swallowed arguments before you could say, "on the other hand." Logic fled out the window. Dogmas tangled with bedrock opinions, usually with plenty of arm-waving, ranging happily from Old Time Religion to Nihilist Revolution.

There were a thousand explanations, all uncomplimentary, of what this crazy new art was all about, and what in God's name would women be wearing next year on their heads if plumes went out? All questions were moot, no subjects taboo, no arguments too specious, everyone got into the act and the more sides to a question the better.

Picnics, rides in the surrey, streetcars, hearthsides, dining tables all made excellent arenas, and on occasion even a handy street corner would do. Often the clashes occurred over teacups; either Oolong or Orange Pekoe properly brewed (and the teapot preheated) was stout enough to stimulate hair-raising discussion.

Guests arrived at our door arguing violently, having met other guests as they walked from the streetcar stop. What began as a friendly enough chat sometimes ended in bitter feuds that might last a year, though my mother was inclined, if that happened, to invite the two adversaries to come together again, with no henchmen, and patch up an agreement.

Was Mr. John D. Rockefeller—"Coal Oil Johnny," as more vehement neighbors called him—a money-grabbing tyrant as Miss Ida Tarbell claimed in *McClure's Magazine?* Was the wild, accidental president, Teddy Roosevelt, with all his talk about malefactors of great wealth, simply trying to lead us down the road to Socialism?

Was it true that Indiana's gas wells, so prodigal all these years down around Muncie, Anderson and little Elwood, might give out any day now, if people didn't turn down the furnace when the house got too hot, instead of merely opening all the windows? Was smallpox vaccination an Anarchist plot, or just a doctor's scheme to pry the last nickel out of our pockets? Should horseless carriages still be held to eight miles an hour on rural roads, or the limit raised to fifteen? And the fine for exceeding it pushed up from a hundred dollars to two hundred, or three hundred on the Sabbath?

If guests forgot to bring their own arguments, my mother could take care of that quickly. She need ask only one question to get discussion rolling. She might inquire innocently of one of our more solid citizens if he thought that Mr. Bill Hosey, that serious-minded machinist over at the Pennsy shops, would make a good mayor.

One lady spilled her tea at that question; one gentleman who disliked scenes suddenly remembered an appointment and fled. But having stirred up a delightful donnybrook, Mother could sit back quietly without saying another word and let the others carry on. For Mr. Hosey—who later was elected mayor several times and made a good one—had come out shockingly for a tax on all incomes, an insanity that made several of our better-heeled and quicker-tempered citizens threaten to move forthwith to Canada. He even dared suggest a municipal lighting plant and elevated railroad tracks.

Most of our more interesting guests leaped into any argument, pro or con, at the drop of a hat, but my parents' good friend Dr. Kent Wheelock was less phlegmatic. He never waited for the hat to drop. A happy warrior and master of polemics, he had a fine, built-in set of patriotic prejudices mounted on hair-springs, and one of the sights in Fort Wayne was the bold doctor in an all-American frenzy taking on vigorously anyone who had dared say, "Yes, but there's another side . . ."

A medical "specialist" who confined his practice to fitting glasses, removing cinders from eyes, tonsils from throats and beans from ears of the very young, he reduced his workload and his income after middle age because there were so many more important things that needed to be done. Writing letters, for example. This was the sturdy patriot who signed "Americus" to the violently libelous letters he sent to the newspapers. Gart Shober's *Labor Times-Herald,* the angry doctor even tried to bar from the mails as a fomenter of revolution.

"Fools," usually "with their feet in the public trough," enraged him daily, and one day in particular it was the Filipinos.

The Spanish-American War had ended gloriously, with the Haughty Don groveling on his knees. The abused Filipinos had been liberated from the cruel-yoke-of-Spain, so now we must pacify them. With guns, of course, bayonets if necessary. It was no fault of ours, Dr. Wheelock argued, that native chief Aguinaldo for some reason didn't want to be ruled by the Americans any more than he had by the Spaniards. It was frightfully ungrateful, now wasn't it? Fancy, their insisting on running their own dirty islands!

My mother's outspoken friend Mrs. Belle Taylor defended the Filipino rebels whenever opportunity presented itself. A woman of solid convictions, a couple of generations later she would have been even busier, torn between her conflicting duties of joining the Peace Corps or picketing the mayor's office while singing that she would overcome.

Independence ran high in her family. Her husband, Sam, a tall man with mutton-chop whiskers, played the pipe organ well, sang basso profundo, tuned pianos—but only for people he liked—and led Catholic, Baptist or Jewish choirs indiscriminately, for a fee of course, whenever they needed his services.

"As for that scoundrel Aguinaldo," Dr. Wheelock went on, "I hope General Freddie Funston will hang him up by his neck."

He had hardly got the last word out when Mrs. Taylor, in a firm clear voice, said that she felt terribly sorry for "our little brown brothers."

The good doctor tipped his head, cupped his right hand to his right ear and asked, "What was that you said?"

"I'm sorry for our little brown brothers," Mrs. Taylor repeated.

Dr. Wheelock's explosion was the loudest our town had heard since a nitroglycerine wagon blew up six years earlier at Hartford City, seventy miles away. It had killed two men and four mules and curdled the milk in the udders of ten thousand innocent cows.

"Brown brothers!" the doctor screamed. "Those heathen monkeys!"

It was that fat-headed un-American radical, Judge William Howard Taft, who first had called them brothers, the doctor stormed. Mrs. Taylor need not repeat it. Taft was not only a fool but a dangerous fool! That hearty chuckle he turned on was misleading. How President McKinley could have picked him to head the Philippines Commission was beyond belief. Rudyard Kipling was the man to listen to about that part of the uncivilized world.

Kipling. Here was a name the younger ones knew. Kipling was the poet for whom we had named our greyhound. But the doctor was not discussing either dogs or poetry.

"The Good Lord ordained that America and Great Britain

assume their responsibilities and rule these lesser breeds without the law!" he shouted. It was our destiny. The lesser breeds were Africans, Filipinos, Sulu Islanders, Chinese and a lot of others just like them. The only way to handle them was through an aggressive policy. Wasn't that what Senator Beveridge was advising, too?

"But they *are* our brothers," Mrs. Taylor persisted. "The Bible says . . ."

"Don't Bible me!" Dr. Wheelock shouted. " 'Every fool lays open his folly.' That's Bible, too. *Proverbs,* if you want to look it up. Brown varmints!"

My mother said, "Tush," and Dr. Wheelock picked up his cup of tea, tasted it, dropped in three lumps of sugar, put the cup down again without drinking, and to no one in particular in his fine, carrying voice began to recite the verse that had made Teddy Roosevelt laugh, even while he scolded the young naval officer who wrote it:

> *"He may be a brother to Big Bill Taft,*
> *But he ain't any brother of mine."*

Another word that ranked with "Aguinaldo" in the give-and-take over afternoon teacups was "transcendentalism." After lying dormant for a number of years, it had cropped up again in discussions in the local churches, a bone, Uncle Gustave said, that the Lutherans out at Concordia College couldn't let lie. One professor had written a letter for publication, and to the general amazement, the Right Rev. John Oechtering of St. Mary's Catholic Church wrote another the next week, agreeing. Both Father Oechtering and the professor condemned to the bottom of Hell the New Englanders who had invented the word.

Some people could not even bring themselves to say "transcendentalism" aloud. Dr. Wagenhals of Trinity English Lutheran Church, who had been so shocked at Uncle Gustave's defense of Darwin, simply called it "Ralph Waldo Emerson's faulty Christianity," which was supposed not only to be easier to say but to understand.

Another guest, who sometimes remained three minutes,

sometimes three hours, was Mr. Henry M. Williams, a handsome gentleman who never raised his voice, no matter how annoyed he became. Unlike Dr. Wheelock with his passionate concern for True Americanism, Mr. Williams let his enthusiasms wander freely and pleasantly over dozens of pet subjects.

He did not paint, did not write poetry, as everyone else in town who had gone through fourth grade was trying to do, and his ideas of art were varied. I went once with my mother and the Misses Jessie and Agnes Hamilton to call on him; it had something to do with a rare book they had discovered. He lived alone in airy but rather Spartan quarters, which we entered to face an oak hatrack, with arms sticking out like the limbs of a tree. On each arm hung a woman's large straw hat, festooned with marigolds, carnations, hyacinths and roses. But no birds. He was a charter member of the Audubon Society and led the local fight against killing birds to put on Nellie's hat. He kept the hats there, for all guests to admire, he explained reasonably, because he thought them much prettier than any picture.

Mr. Williams' ideas at tea time were often as unexpected as the hats. He didn't set out to be original, but he usually was. For years he had been absorbed in the subject of transportation, by which now he meant the state's new interurban electric railroads. He hadn't held the reins on the first run of the first horse-drawn streetcar, my mother used to say, but he would have liked to, and he had sat in the first coach and the horses almost ran away.

When horse-drawn cars were gone, he became eloquent about electricity. It was regrettable, he had admitted—very well, amusing, he amended when Mother smiled—regrettable that the traction company's first car over one line had to be hauled by a steam locomotive, but that would not happen again. He would see to it.

Mr. Williams always sat very straight, as an old soldier should. Forty years after the Civil War he still carried himself in a military manner, though he never wore a G. A. R. hat as most of his comrades did. His friends expected him to talk about transportation. What they did not expect, a day the younger generation was passing the tea, was for him to startle everyone suddenly by linking our town to Athens.

"Future generations," he said positively, "will equate the Indiana of today with ancient Greece."

He did not offer proof or even explain how that happy situation would come about, but Indiana, this very minute, was in the midst of a Golden Age.

If it were evening when company was at the house and Uncle Gustave were home, it was he who did any needling, just to keep the conversation spicy, he always explained. If he were not home, it was Mother. She never was lax as a hostess, but neither did she pass up a good chance for discussion, and now she asked Mr. Williams if he thought Sappho and Homer were living in the Wabash Valley today?

No, Mr. Williams said, taking her seriously. They weren't. But James Whitcomb Riley lived on Lockerby Street in Indianapolis. Mrs. Gene Stratton Porter in Geneva, just thirty-eight miles straight south. And General Lew Wallace in Crawfordsville.

"And this new fellow Meredith Nicholson, down at Indianapolis," he warmed to his subject. "His novel's a best seller. Calls it *The House of a Thousand Candles*. Not only written in Indiana by a son of our state, but all the incidents happen right over around Lake Maxinkuckee.

"And the McCutcheon boys. Two in one family, and one of them inventing a whole kingdom, Graustark, so real the New York steamship lines have to explain they can't sell tickets to it!"

Mr. Williams proceeded to make other important points. He was proud of his state. Its authors were turning out more best-selling books than other authors anywhere. He could prove it. Hoosiers were writing plays, histories, hymns, poetry. They were dancing like angels, composing music, building architectural gems. Those were approximately his words.

"Well, perhaps not architectural gems," he conceded.

My mother, in the tone that never revealed whether she was amused or impressed, asked when this Golden Age started.

"In the last days of President Ben Harrison's administration.

Remember, he was a Hoosier, too," Mr. Williams replied promptly. There had been no fanfare. The peak years were underway when the battleship *Maine* sank.

"Look at Senator Albert Beveridge," he added. "A better speaker than Chauncey DePew. More style."

Mother admitted that. She did not agree with all of Senator Beveridge's ideas, on Manifest Destiny in the Phillipines among others. But he was a gentleman and a fine orator. My father had voted for him, impressed by his flow of elegant words. Impressing me was his four-inch starched collar, taller even than Uncle Gustave's.

"Try copying his manners," Mother had told me one day, "try to talk as well as he does," and she showed me a line from a Chicago paper. In Mr. Finley Peter Dunne's column, Mr. Dooley, talking about Senator Beveridge's oratory, had said, "Ye c'ld waltz to it."

After Mr. Williams found his hat, said, "Good afternoon, ladies," and started slowly for the streetcar, and with that as a signal the rest of the guests had departed, Mother poured herself another cup of tea and sipped it slowly.

"State pride is splendid," she said finally, "a beautiful thing. Where would we be without it? Living in mud and still fighting Indians, I suppose. But it never pays to take one's self and one's environment too seriously.

"I am always reminded of what Mr. Riley said one day at a lecture on art in Indianapolis. The speaker had talked too long; everyone was restless. When he finally finished, Mr. Riley turned to a friend and said, 'Speakin' of art, I know a feller over at Terry Haute that kin spit clean over a boxcar.'"

16

THE BANDS PLAY ON

FOR SEVERAL YEARS, Mr. Henry Berghoff, our distinguished mayor and a member of the local family that brewed Dortmunder beer, handled all formal occasions in our town. He had several advantages, even before he pulled down his fashionable white vest, cleared his throat and said, "Ladies and Gentlemen, and Fellow Citizens All."

To begin with, Mr. Berghoff looked important. His stiff gates-ajar collar, gray striped pants and frock coat with white carnation always seemed brand new, as if they had come within the hour from a rack in Mr. Reuben S. Patterson's or Mr. Golden's Gentlemen's Clothing and Furnishing stores. His silver-colored hair he wore in a Bismarckian brush and the spikes on his graying mustaches were the sharpest upturned saber points this side of Potsdam.

To my mother's satisfaction, my Republican father had voted for Mr. Berghoff in the latest election, despite the damning fact that he was an Eighth Ward Democrat and had been endorsed almost unanimously by that hotbed of revolution, the Fort Wayne Federation of Labor at its regular monthly meeting in Harmony Hall.

Mr. Berghoff won, and not by a hair. By a whopping plurality he defeated handsome young Captain Charley Reese,

Commander of the Fort Wayne Rifles, newly returned from heroic, if bloodless, Spanish-American War service at Camp Chickamauga Park and Port Tampa, Florida.

Everyone knew that it had not been Captain Charley's fault that he and his boys were left behind while other companies sailed to Cuba. They had developed not only malaria but also dysentery from the scandalous "embalmed beef" sold to the Army by the Chicago stockyards. The Captain's veterans campaigned for him vigorously. He was charming, people said, but what was his experience in the job of running a growing city?

Mr. Berghoff, on the other hand, had held public office. He had served as city treasurer, and not only was supposed to keep all the books in order, but actually did. Also, even with Captain Reese to compete with, he had been a hero in his own right.

Voters remembered the unhappy day when the city's street-car conductors and motormen, some eighty-five in all, whom most citizens always had considered loyal, friendly and patriotic, went out on strike. One pair even left a Belt Line car standing in the middle of the Transfer Corner at Main and Calhoun Streets, as a symbol, unkind people said, of their knavish disregard for human rights.

Sheriff Ed Clausmeier, a man of decision, called at once for volunteers to serve as deputy sheriffs. His action startled the strikers, most of whom were quiet, if desperate, middle-aged men, who were enjoying their respite from fifteen-hour days by sitting at ease, drinking beer, in Mr. Jimmy Riley's Sample Room, just around the corner from the car barns. It never had occurred to them to plan violent revolution. They merely wanted a raise from thirteen and a half to fifteen cents an hour.

Mr. Berghoff was one of the first volunteers to strap on his pearl-handled pistol, take the oath to defend the Constitution, and guard the Chestnut Street car barns and powerhouse from lawless fellows throwing eggs. Several dozen stalwart citizens joined him—Mr. Henry Paul, six feet three inches of incorruptible banker; thin, sparse-haired, nearsighted Mr. Charley

Woodworth, the popular druggist whose shop was in the corner of the Aveline House; even highly respected and conservative Mr. Charley McCulloch, whose father had been Lincoln's Secretary of the Treasury. The only Democrat besides Mr. Berghoff in the group was Mr. Moses Lamley, the quiet gentleman who in his shop on Harrison Street sold the best *gefuelter fisch* and kosher sausages to be found in Indiana.

Naturally the deputies, including even Mr. McCulloch, were willing to forget the Democratic label on their comrade-in-arms and they worked hard for him. He did not disappoint them after his election. He almost neglected the brewery to attend dinners, luncheons, church benefits and committee meetings at City Hall.

On special days when the band finished "The Star-Spangled Banner" and Mayor Berghoff stepped forward to speak, no one ever heard a more patriotic talk. He eulogized the settlers in the wilderness, harrassed by mosquitoes, Indians and rattle-snakes, who met at Corydon years before to write a State Constitution. He described how, with long rifles loaded, they had argued under the elm at Big Indian Creek over slavery, the poll tax, free schools, tolls, and which were better, roads or canals.

"God bless the brave founders of our state," Mayor Berghoff always concluded.

Everyone agreed. Only an uninformed newcomer in Indiana would neglect to honor the founders. Seldom, even in the stress and hurly-burly of changing times, was any important person or red-letter date overlooked.

This had happened once, however, the year before Poet Riley used me as a prop at the Princess Rink, when the city fathers, to their deep embarrassment, forgot to observe the town's one hundredth anniversary. They couldn't downgrade General Anthony Wayne, so they celebrated it the next fall with a glorious week of festivities filled with military drills and salutes, sham battles between Indians and settlers, a parade five miles long, flags, transparencies, kerosene torches, sparklers, pink candy, boys running wild, boys held in leash by their parents, babies in buggies.

This was an era of parades, the bigger the better, and horses dominated them, not automobiles. Once, after elephants in a Ringling Brothers circus frightened a farmer's horse and it bolted into the crowd and killed a woman, our enlightened town council drew up an ordinance prohibiting elephants and camels, but not bolting horses. It was discriminating, some of us thought. How would one ever see a camel at close hand if not in a circus parade? One could always see horses. The automobile had not yet retired them.

"Horseless carriages" were just curiosities that you stared at, but seldom got a chance to ride in; and certainly they would not be safe in a parade, with people walking in the street. The year I started to school, an adventurous architect named Henry Meyer surprised his friends by buying an automobile. Mr. Erastus B. Kunkle, the valve manufacturer, invested in the next one, and then Mr. Will Peltier, the bicycle-riding undertaker.

Mr. Kunkle was a spectacular-looking man. He had a large waxed black mustache and all the time his hair kept getting whiter, the mustache stayed black. He had come to our railroad town as a locomotive mechanic and gotten rich by inventing a safety lock for engines. His plant on Barr Street, back of City Hall, always smelled deliciously of engine oil. He did not welcome boys inside the building; he had the foolish idea someone might get hurt. But we could look in the window, and if we were driven away doing that, there was always one solace. We could run around the corner to the Patrol Wagon barn.

Mr. Kunkle's little, black, open, one-seater had only one small headlight in the middle of its front, but Mr. Peltier's had four, a pair of kerosene side lanterns and two Prestolite headlamps that burned carbide gas and constantly threatened to blow up.

Two or three years earlier, Mr. Elwood Haynes had brought his new gasoline car up to Fort Wayne. My father took me downtown to see the contraption, on display on Calhoun Street in the neighborhood of the Cathedral and Louis Jocquel's stationery store. A handful of boys was allowed to try the leather seat for a minute. It was exciting, no one would admit it was scary. Disappointingly, it did not look as sure of covering the ground as my father's bicycle, and it was considerably noisier.

Mr. Haynes had driven to Fort Wayne from Kokomo on his car's bicycle tires over mud roads at five to ten miles an hour. He went on to Chicago later to join a few other gas "buggies" and a couple of electrics in an "endurance" run of fifty miles. He reached Chicago safely enough but did not get into the race. For, before its start, he ran into a streetcar and smashed one of his spindly wheels.

Everybody was mildly sorry, for the state's entry in any contest should win, but it was no personal disappointment. Automobiles were not a part of the daily scene. Let those ride who wanted. It was much more exhilarating to tramp down the street behind the National Guard Artillery Regiment's Military Band playing Sousa's "Washington Post." What did it matter or who cared if the recruit not yet in uniform playing the slide trombone in the back row was out of step and out of key?

It was a poor excuse of a town that failed to send at least one lively band to join a neighboring town's celebration. They came to honor old soldiers, young soldiers, dead soldiers, General Lawton on his way from the Pacific for burial, past governors, present governors, dedication of the Spanish guns captured in Cuba and the Philippines.

The Hiberian Rifles displayed their new uniforms, the Zollinger Battery its three-inch guns. The Fort Wayne Rifles wore their blue outfits with white cross-belts; the Scottish Rite Masons, most of whom were too old to march, wore their white ostrich plumes and swords; the Modern Woodmen had their nickle-plated axes. Even the band from the School for Feeble-minded Children was in line on special occasions, and no one objected if they didn't keep step.

Heroic martial gentlemen, no longer young, seized the excuse to squeeze themselves into outgrown uniforms and mount rambunctious charges that had not been saddled frequently in late years. Gentlemen and horses both were applauded loudly, not only because the gentlemen were the Brave-Men-Who-Saved-the-Union-God-Bless-Them, but because the excitement and alarums that their mounts created made any parade worthwhile. Unaccustomed to the feel of cold steel against their rumps, or startled at a sour note on Mr. Schober's cornet, the horses would rear up and take off, with or without their riders. The only thing more exciting than a riderless horse threatening to trample women or children was one with a splendidly uniformed rider, his medals flapping and his arms around the beast's neck, trying desperately to hang on.

If you were too old or too dignified or too young to march, you watched from the sidewalk or ran along the edge, always in some way taking part actively. This was especially true if the rally had to do with politics. People put on their hats, and carrying a flag on a stick under an arm, joined the mob on the street and sang "The Battle Hymn of the Republic" feelingly. After reaching Princess Rink or Court House Square or wherever the event might be, they listened attentively, cheered or jeered, and went home exhausted but afire to discuss what the hero or rascal had said, or did not say and should have.

Candidates and casualties were of every shade: Republicans and Democrats, four hundred and ninety-nine persistant Populists, a handful of die-hard Greenbackers, remnants of this splinter group or that—and two or three times a year the dangerous man from Terre Haute, Mr. Eugene Debs, put in an appearance.

Hanging around the edges of local events, I saw the fiery Mr. Debs several times. Once he was addressing an enthusiastic meeting of the Brotherhood of Railroad Firemen and Engineers in Harmony Hall, above the saloon on West Berry Street with the plump, naked ladies painted on the wall above the bar. A friend, the son of a labor-union officer, smuggled me into the back row and we stuck the speech out.

Another time Mr. Debs stood on the platform of the Pennsylvania station, eating a ham sandwich, hat off, sweat and cinders showing on his bald head, waiting for the engine that had hauled the train from Crestline to limp off to the shop and a shining new one to back in to relieve it. Mr. Debs walked up and down while he waited, his face in smiles one moment, clouding up the next, then smiling again. He handed everyone in sight a copy of *Appeal to Reason* and I took mine home for my parents to read.

"He brushes the cobwebs off people's minds," my mother said after she had looked at it.

She was against cobwebs and I suspect had a sneaking admiration for the old Socialist. She was one of the few in our town who did. Debs was one subject on which the *News*, the *Sentinel*, the *Journal Gazette* and the two German dailies, the *Staats-Zeitung* and the *Abendpost*, could agree. They thought he belonged in jail, were delighted when he did go there and shocked when behind bars he polled four million votes for President.

There was a saying around Indiana that any smart boy with hard work and a bit of luck could become a poet, a best-selling novelist, a composer of gospel hymns or barroom ballads—and if through his own sloth he failed in these ambitions, he could always run for Vice-President and sometimes be elected. Before my generation, Mr. Schuyler Colfax served with General Grant as Vice-President and Mr. Thomas Hendricks was elected once with President Cleveland. In my own time the two Hoosiers elected Vice-President were chilly Mr. Charles Fairbanks and the spindly prosecutor from Whitley County, Mr. Tom Marshall.

My father took me to a rally at the Princess Rink once when Mr. Fairbanks was running for the Senate. He spoke earnestly at some length, but without setting the bunting afire. I had been shocked while we were walking down Main Street to the meeting to hear my father tell the friend with him, "Poor Charley Fairbanks has ice water in his veins."

I accepted the remark literally, particularly after the speech. Mr. Fairbanks was a tall, thin, straight-shouldered, unsmiling man with a shiny, bald head; and he wore the usual hard-starched collar around a thin neck and a sprout of well-trimmed, dark, chin whiskers. He was elected, then re-elected, and my father voted for him. Though later, when he was T.R.'s running mate for his second term, my Republican

parent, still uneasy, admitted that the very thought of Charley
Fairbanks in the White House was enough to make all sensible
Americans pray nightly for the continued health of Mr. Roose-
velt.

The town treated Mr. Fairbanks politely, but homespun
Tom Marshall it took to its heart. My recollection of the future
Vice-President on the days he came up from his Columbia
City law office is of a big, black hat, creased fore and aft and
tilted slightly to the right, on a big, fine-boned head atop an
agile, little body, with elbows thrust out like a cricket. His
voice did not have Senator Beveridge's butter. It was more like
the twang of a country barber-shop guitar—not gritty. The
word "gritty" was reserved in our neighborhood for an auc-
tioneer running for governor. His oratory, the *Journal Gazette*
reported, broke all windows in the block.

Marshall talked less than did most of the men around him.
Somewhere, hobnobbing with lawyers, editors and complaining citizens, he had learned what my father called the difficult
art of being a good listener. Governor, Vice-President twice,
he was a little like Secretary of State Hay who wrote the
amusing poem about "Little Breeches" and was remembered
as much for it as for more important achievements. In Mr.
Marshall's case, it was the eleven words he uttered one day to
the clerk of the Senate. Bored with a dreary debate, the Vice-
President whispered, "What this country needs most is a good
five-cent cigar."

Once, early one rainy Saturday morning in the Wabash Railroad baggage room, I saw Democrats Marshall and Meredith
Nicholson in a political huddle with candidate-for-President
William Jennings Bryan. Sitting on the edge of a baggage
truck, I watched the three great men talk. Big, paunchy Mr.
Bryan had got off an early train from Toledo, and as usual he
was hungry. Someone had brought a package of salami sand-
wiches from Mr. McKinney's Eating House, and Mr. Bryan
was wolfing them down. Lawyer Marshall and Author Nicholson, who was to be a polished diplomat later, were both on the
thin side and were not eating. They were too busy saving the
country for their party to think of food.

Our county liked Bryan. It usually voted Democratic for President, even for Cleveland over Hoosier Harrison, chiefly because of the heavy vote by the men in the shops. Bryan drew immense crowds in *Sängerbund Halle* or the Princess Rink whenever he came to speak. In elections he drew majorities over both McKinley and Taft.

Citizens, including my mother, complained a great deal about the electric power company. Rates and profits were high, service poor, they thought, and Bryan, like future Mayor Hosey, gave them encouragement. But Mr. Bryan's ideas on prohibition didn't set well with a beer-loving community or a whiskey-drinking author, and this morning in the Wabash station, Mr. Nicholson was arguing with Mr. Bryan. Mr. Marshall was listening.

It was all right for a Presidential candidate to ask if God or Nature or Man were responsible for the Trusts, Mr. Nicholson was insisting loudly. Prohibition was fine and dandy for anyone who did not want a drink. But it was bad politics in this part of Indiana. Couldn't Mr. Bryan stay off the subject the few hours he was here?

In the years of my growing up, five or six governors served their single, and in some cases undistinguished, two-year terms in the State House at Indianapolis. They were barred by law from succeeding themselves, no matter how much money they saved the taxpayers. Or, confusingly to me, how much they had banked.

That they stashed away something for themselves, in some mysterious way, I was forced to believe because one day in Uncle Martin's drug store I heard a distinguished member of the legislature tell him, "If a governor can't pocket enough in two years, he's not much of a governor."

"Rubbish," my mother said.

I was convinced, however, that of all the great men who came to town, the governors led the most fascinating lives. They were always on the go somewhere in the state, always on hand to lay cornerstones while the bands played, at what the *Evening News* referred to in a spirit of awe as "impressive ceremonies," and the *Evening Sentinel* as "mammoth displays of pageantry."

The governor always had the best and biggest chair on the platform and rode ahead of everybody else in one of Mr. Barnett's better carriages, with the top down. They wore plug hats, stylish Prince Albert coats, in season the usual flowers in their buttonholes, and were responsible more than anyone else, I was convinced, for the fact that one could watch the "impressive ceremonies" without having to buy a ticket.

17

SCHOLAR IN A
SHOE SHOP

❋⤙✧⤚❋⤙✧⤚❋⤙✧⤚❋⤙✧⤚❋⤙✧⤚❋⤙✧⤚❋⤙✧⤚❋⤙✧⤚❋⤙✧⤚❋⤙✧⤚❋⤙✧⤚❋⤙✧⤚

JOHN JACOBS was an old man when I was a small boy. He ran a little shoe store on Calhoun Street and owned what was said to be one of the finest private libraries in the state. Each night, after fitting shoes all day, he hurried home to that library, and by the light of two kerosene lamps read the *Odes of Horace* or some other classic aloud to his wife, Sarah, and on Sunday afternoons to as many lucky boys as had gathered to listen.

In the book-lined library or on the long porch at the rear of the house, through Mr. Jacobs' eyes boys met the Roman Empire face to face. William of Normandy swaggered on English soil and the year 1066 became important. They met fire-breathing Tom Paine. They heard the cold blade of the guillotine fall in the *Place de la Concorde,* as I had been told my own great grandmother had heard it, when as a schoolgirl she was led by pious nuns to witness the end of that bad, bad man Robespierre.

We listened while Mr. Jacobs read a passage from Virgil or Schopenhauer or from the Bible. Whatever it was, no matter how long ago written, it seemed of vital importance. He read to us in English, of course. If we could have understood, he might have preferred Greek or Latin, French or German,

Italian or Spanish. Sanscrit, he admitted, sometimes gave him pause and he usually had trouble with Arabic; "but in translations," he said, "you lose too much beauty."

Below the porch where we sat, Spy Run chattered past, a talkative little creek canopied by great oaks and walnut trees, making a murmuring accompaniment to the old man's voice. The Spy Run Avenue streetcar line passed the gate at the foot of the hill and ended its run almost directly opposite the front door of Mr. Jacobs' shoe store. He rarely used the streetcar. He pumped the mile and a half into town on his bicycle, with a split-stave basket wired to the handlebars, and if it were raining, a large umbrella overhead. He was frank about the reason for the bicycle. Using it, he saved a nickel each way, to put into travel or books.

In the basket he carried his lunch, whatever book he happened to be reading, and usually a dozen or two fresh eggs. These he gathered, often by lantern light, in the early morning at the henhouse below his home on the hill, and he sold them to special highly privileged friends and customers for one cent a dozen more than they would have had to pay at Mr. Ditto's Fancy Grocery. For the penny, the buyer got assurance that today's eggs actually were today's.

Mr. Jacobs was a fairly tall, big-boned man with a knotty face and bloodshot eyes, and he wore a sparse growth of chin whisker. In winter he was bundled in a heavy overcoat; on his head he wore a black cloth cap with earmuffs turned down, and around his neck a thick woolen shawl with its ends blowing in the wind. He got up early. He believed in a solid breakfast, and the shop had to be opened promptly at eight o'clock.

Saturdays it remained open until eleven, but on weekdays, summer or winter, one saw its proprietor standing impatiently in the doorway, the big brass key in his hand, listening for the six o'clock church bells to ring. The Catholics were a little more prompt or a little more sure of themselves. They rang first and the others chimed in a few heartbeats later. Mr. Jacobs was a Lutheran, but at the first Catholic peal he turned the key in the door and his back on business and went home to his library. He never waited for the Lutheran bells.

His library was not the largest in town. One heard that it was, but this was untrue, my mother said. Perhaps a dozen other persons had more books by count on their shelves: Bishop Herman Alerding, the Rev. Samuel Wagenhals, Miss Margaret Hamilton, Mrs. Will Fleming, Mr. Holman Hamilton with five thousand. Mr. Jacobs kept his pruned to fifteen hundred. He bought, read, reread and then evaluated. Was the new book better than some older one on the shelves? If so, the older went, unless it happened to be rare.

For years the Public Library had hundreds of books in its catalogues that originally had been Mr. Jacobs'. The Railroad Y.M.C.A., the city high school, Concordia Lutheran College, the Catholic Library, all profited. So also did friends. It was not uncommon to see Mr. Jacobs' bicycle leaning against a hitching post while he went to a friend's door and said, "Here's Montaigne on the education of children. Keep it."

The Jacobs Shoe Store, dingy and never brightly lighted except for the Welsbach burner in the gas jet over his book-strewn desk, was four or five doors north of the Transfer Corner on the east side of Calhoun Street. All streetcar lines met at that point, with Tony Lintz, the major domo, throwing the switches with his long iron bar, to send the cars in the proper directions. Passengers, alighting with transfers, continued up or down or across town on the original nickel fare. If quick, they could even stop off to do a bit of shopping.

The Transfer Corner was as near a Times Square or Piccadilly Circus as the town had. Al Alter's Cigar Store was on one corner, Cooney Bayer's Cigars and the Court House and Hamilton National Bank on the other three. Families that wanted plain, substantial shoes and galoshes went into the Jacobs store; children went alone if that were more convenient, for parents could trust Mr. John Jacobs to fit them right at the right price.

If you wanted high style, you went up the street another four blocks to Mr. App's. Mr. App wore patent-leather shoes and a watered silk cravat and perhaps the first pair of rimless glasses in town, and bowed from the waist to every customer. He was a reckless merchant, who went out on a limb to break the top price barrier: he introduced Stacey-Adams shoes for men at a whopping three dollars a pair. There was no such foolishness about John Jacobs. He measured a foot, fitted it, and said, "Sorry, the price has gone up to a dollar seventy-five."

Mr. Jacobs had been a student in Oberlin College when the Civil War began and he enlisted. Promoted to lieutenant, then captain, he led a company in the capture of Island Number Ten in the Mississippi and drove a Confederate force into the swamps in Tennessee. He had malaria, dysentery, and jaundice; his commanding officer found him lying in the rain and "furloughed him home to die."

Recovery was slow. A pacifist, he hated war, but a sense of duty to country and decency to comrades drove him back again into uniform; and with General Sherman he marched through Georgia to the sea.

After the war he finished school at Oberlin before he came to Fort Wayne with his father. Helping organize the first G.A.R. post, he listed himself as a lieutenant, a pretense he kept up all his life. "Too many captains and colonels around," he said. "I'm contented as a lieutenant." Another such "contented" veteran, he discovered before long, was Mr. Eli Hoffman, the hardwood lumberman, who lived in a big red-stone house with two round towers on West Berry Street and who at a G.A.R. meeting, where fellow veterans all seemed to be men of rank, announced, "I was the only private in the army and I'm proud of it."

Mr. Jacobs resigned from the G.A.R. when what he thought were veterans' greedy attacks on the public treasury annoyed him. He refused a pension—"it was a money grab"—and years later when Congress made pensions obligatory to all veterans, he signed his check over each month to a person or institution he believed needed it more than he did.

I lived across town from Spy Run and on Sunday afternoons I might ride my bicycle out to the Jacobs' hill, sometimes alone. It did not occur to me at the time that to reach the quiet of his library I was passing through a world foreign to it. I'd push my bicycle north, across the Nickel Plate tracks, past the Palms Sample Room with its sign over the back door that said, "Family Entrance." Then north along the wooden fence of the Central League baseball park. There I paused long enough to learn the score from someone looking through a knothole and paused again to glance toward Eureka Street, where a row of houses backed up against the county jail were called the "Jail Flats." Women in kimonos sat in rows on the porches, rocking and shouting to passersby. I never ventured too close to them.

Near the hill, Mr. Louis Centlivre's old French Brewery loomed up on the right, with the heroic bronze statue of the original Centlivre on the roof, mustached, frock-coated, plump and vastly dignified, his left foot firmly planted on a beer keg. "Stepping heavenward," my mother always called it.

One Sunday Mr. Jacobs began to talk about Russia. I had heard my parents that week discussing a story in the local papers about an uprising put down successfully by Czarist troops. Mr. Jacobs was excited and disturbed.

"You can't heal a running sore by covering it with a sticking plaster," he said. "A revolution will start in Russia. Revolutions always start where the pressure from above is heaviest. In twenty years, thirty perhaps, it will come. It will trouble the world."

Another day he folded his newspaper carefully—it was the *Boston Transcript*—wiped his glasses vigorously, pointed them at me and remarked, "Women are people, aren't they? They are reasoning animals. Why shouldn't they vote?"

His wife looked startled and he demanded, "You have intelligence, haven't you, Sarah? Is there any reason you should be classed with the cattle in the cattle barn?"

Once on the rear porch he read Dickens aloud to a pair of us. The sun was shining and it was spring and down at the foot of the hill Spy Run was tumbling noisily over a spillway and beyond the river, in Louis Centlivre's Driving Park, men were exercising their horses in impromptu harness races.

There were catfish in Spy Run. The green fields were ripe

for exploration. The horses rounding the curve on the race track called to us with hooves that sounded like hands clapping. But with none of their usual appeal to us, for Mr. Jacobs was reading Dickens.

At last he put the book back precisely in its place on a shelf and said, "A great man, Dickens. A bad novelist, if you ask me. But a great social reformer. He sought to end injustice. The way to end it is through reasoning. But reason runs into a wall of prejudice and habit. So the true reformer forgets reason and attacks the emotions. That's what Dickens did."

His wife knit as she listened, her thin, white hands working rapidly. Only once did I see her angry.

That time she called him out of the room, and I could hear her voice scolding him. It was a day in winter and Mr. Jacobs had taken me for a walk down across the fields to see a sick horse a farmer was nursing in a stable somewhere beyond Spy Run. The wind was biting, and when we came in his wife had hot tea and cookies waiting for us.

John Jacobs was cold. Instead of taking a cup of tea, he puttered a moment in the kitchen, then appeared with two little glasses of a sweet red liquid and gave me one of them. I gulped mine. It was warm and good.

I saw Mrs. Jacobs staring at him with color in her cheeks.

"I'll speak to you outside," she said.

In the hallway I could hear her telling him that he should be ashamed, giving wine to a mere twelve-year-old. I had liked it, but he never gave me any more.

One day he handed me a shabby volume and told me that perhaps I was too young for it, but to try to read it. I did and understood enough to realize why he presented it. It was *Children of the Ghetto,* by Israel Zangwill, a brutal story of smoldering resentment in a London slum. It had created a stir in England some years before, with cooler heads persuading the House of Lords not to order it burned. Mother had never had it on her bookshelves until Mr. Jacobs' copy arrived. She had read it and sympathized but found the literary style appalling. No amount of truth, Mother believed, could excuse bad writing.

Mr. and Mrs. Jacobs visited our house occasionally with other guests. The discussions were always lively. They concerned the Romanoffs once, and the part they played in fomenting Polish pogroms. Dr. Nelson Lloyd Deming defended the pogrom as an institution, to the shock of Mr. Jacobs, and he bent his head forward to look coldly at Dr. Deming over his steel-rimmed spectacles and said, "You ought to be ashamed of yourself, sir," and repeated it, "You ought to be ashamed!"

Once every four or five years, Mr. Jacobs locked the shoe store for two or three months, hired a farmer from up the road to look after his house and his chickens, and with his wife took off for adventure in far places. His egg money paid part of the cost, his shrewd investments the rest. He sold shoes too reasonably for there to be much profit from the store.

Returning from the trip, he might exclaim, "We have been to Carcassonne! The poets say it better than I can. See Carcassonne and die! There's nothing more to see!"

One of his summers in Greece was memorable. Reading at home, he had found errors in translations from certain Greek classics, and had to make sure with his own eyes. So he paced the Acropolis, then carried his findings to the Greek Department of Antiquities. There was quite a fuss. An American merchant discovering scholars' incompetence! A savant!

In Athens, Editor Bliss Perry of the *Atlantic Monthly*, an English professor at Harvard, came across an elderly couple excitedly measuring an ancient ruin. The old gentleman, later described by Editor Perry as "a man of great diligence and splendid background in Greek history," was talking in ancient Greek to a group of historians from the University. A few weeks later in the Roman Forum, here was the same old couple, this time with classicists from the Vatican in tow. The American's Latin was as fluent as his Greek had been in Athens.

Curious, Editor Perry followed Mr. Jacobs to his hotel. What was his university?

"University?" Mr. John Jacobs answered. "I'm a merchant."

Editor Perry repeated, "Merchant?"

"Yes, I run a shoe store at Fort Wayne, Indiana, and I'm going back there tomorrow. My fall stock will soon be coming in."

In his autobiography, Editor Perry describes the chance meeting as one of the most interesting in his life. There were boys in Fort Wayne who would have understood.

In early August, 1895, a month before my fourth birthday, I was allowed to go alone the three blocks to my Uncle Martin's drug store. Before me is a clipping from the *Evening Sentinel* of that afternoon:

> An exciting runaway accident occurred near the corner of Calhoun and Holman Streets this morning. A single horse, hitched to an unoccupied carriage in front of the Third Presbyterian Church, became frightened and broke the hitching strap. The animal leaped into the air madly, rushed down Calhoun Street, mounted the sidewalk in front of the Goldstine Second-Hand Store and struck showcases filled with collars, cuffs and artificial flowers. The showcases were wrecked and the goods ruined.
>
> Mr. August Detzer's little son barely escaped with his life.

Think of what I would have missed! Mr. John Jacobs, Buffalo Bill, Aunt Maggie on the back fence, and The Man Who Stole The Bible. Among others.